Contents

Letter to Students...2

Letter to Parents...3

Chapter One: What is the SSAT?.....................................5-7

What is the Purpose of the SSAT?.....................................5

How is the SSAT Designed? 5

The SSAT is Reliable 6

The SSAT is a Norm-Referenced Test.................................6

The SSAT is a Standardized Test..6

Should I Guess on the SSAT?..7

Chapter Two: About the Upper Level SSAT 9-56

The Parts of the Upper Level Test 9-11

The Writing Sample..12-13

The Quantitative Sections 14-15

Quantitative Sample Questions...16-35

The Reading Comprehension Section.................................36-39

Reading Comprehension Sample Questions.......................40-42

The Verbal Section: Synonyms..43-44

Prefixes, Suffixes, and Roots 45-48

Synonym Sample Questions..49

The Verbal Section: Analogies..50-53

Analogy Sample Questions..54-55

Summing It Up 56

Chapter Three: Scores 57-60

What Your Scores Mean...57

Formula Scoring 57

What Do Admission Officers Consider?..............................58

The Score Report...58-60

Parent's Corner: Supporting Your Test Taker 61

Practice Test I 63-99

Practice Test II 100-132

Evaluating Your Upper Level SSAT 133-142

How Did You Do? 134

Scoring the Practice Tests 134

Computing Your Raw Score...135

Answer Keys 136-141

Equating Raw Scores to Scaled Scores..............................142

Dear Students,

The private schools you'll find in books and on television may be interesting, but the real world of independent schools is even more amazing. You're reading this guide right now because you think that an independent school might be right for you, and you're ready for one of the first steps—taking the SSAT.

This book will introduce you to the SSAT, the test format, and what to expect on test day. It contains practice tests that resemble the one you'll be taking, plus preparation tips to help you do your best on the SSAT.

***The Official Guide to the SSAT* gives you:**

- The definition of an admission test

- Descriptions of the test sections

- Test-taking strategies

- Plenty of sample questions to practice

- Two full-length practice tests

- Information about how to interpret scores

- Registration and test day checklists

What won't you find here? Shortcuts, tricks, or gimmicks ("when in doubt, C wins out"). This is the only book that contains sample questions and practice tests written by SSAT test writers and the official test-taking strategies to help you to do your best. There are some valuable hints that can help you stay on track and maximize your time. But when it comes down to it, getting familiar with the test format and scoring, studying specific content covered on the test, and solving practice questions is the best way to prepare for the SSAT.

The path ahead will be exciting, and you'll probably learn a lot about yourself on the way. We wish you the best as you prepare for this journey that will help you apply to a school that will change your life. This book can help you get there.

The Secondary School Admission Test Board (SSATB)

Dear Parents,

Congratulations on your decision to explore an independent school education for your child! For more than 50 years, the SSAT has been the standard in admission testing for the world's best independent schools. We know that the process of taking the SSAT can be fraught with concern and distress, but it needn't be. The SSAT is one important step on the road to an independent school education—one which should be taken seriously, but should not cause undue anxiety.

The results of admission testing, while integral to an application, are just one of many factors considered by admission officers when determining if your child and their schools make a great match. The degree of emphasis placed on scores depends on the school and on other information, such as transcripts and teacher recommendations. For the vast majority of schools, students with a wide range of SSAT scores are admitted.

Here are a few questions that admission officers contemplate when reviewing an applicant's scores:

- Are the scores consistent with the student's academic record?
- Do the scores highlight areas of academic strength or weakness?
- How do these scores compare with those of other students in the applicant pool?
- How do these scores compare with students who have enrolled over the last few years?

As a parent, you have a central role to play in helping your child succeed in the school application process by reminding them to keep the SSAT in perspective. Schools are most interested in finding out who your child is.

There are a multitude of sources, both on- and offline, that promise to prepare your child for the SSAT and increase his/her test score. SSATB does not endorse any test preparation company, individual, or book; even those classes given by our member schools are not sanctioned by our organization. Written by our test development team, this guide was created to support your student's preparation efforts with legitimate information, test-taking strategies, and practice tests. We encourage you to use this guide as your official source for SSAT preparation.

Finally, we encourage you to use the ssat.org website not only to register your child for the test, but also to access information about the independent school application process and search for schools that are the right fit for your child and your family.

We hope this *Official Guide to the Upper Level SSAT* will help to make your family's experience of testing and applying to independent school a successful and enjoyable one.

Good luck!

Heather Hoerle
Executive Director

THIS PAGE INTENTIONALLY LEFT BLANK.

Chapter One:
What is the SSAT?

What is the Purpose of the SSAT?

The SSAT is designed for students who are seeking entrance to independent schools worldwide. The purpose of the SSAT is to measure the basic verbal, quantitative, and reading skills students develop over time—skills that are needed for successful performance in independent schools. The SSAT provides independent school admission professionals with meaningful information about the possible academic success of potential students like you at their institutions, regardless of students' background or experience.

The SSAT is not an achievement test. Your most recent classroom math test, for example, was probably an achievement test: Your teacher specifically designed it to evaluate how much you know about what had been covered in class. The SSAT, on the other hand, is designed to measure the verbal, quantitative, and reading skills you have acquired, instead of focusing on your mastery of particular course materials.

Further, SSAT tests are not designed to measure other characteristics, such as motivation, persistence, or creativity, that may contribute to your success in school.

How is the SSAT Designed?

The SSAT measures three constructs: verbal, quantitative, and reading skills that students develop over time, both in and out of school. It emphasizes critical thinking and problem-solving skills that are essential for academic success.

The overall difficulty level of the SSAT is built to be at 50%-60%. The distribution of question difficulties is set so that the test will effectively differentiate among test takers, who vary in their level of abilities.

In developing the SSAT, the SSATB convenes review committees composed of content experts and independent school teachers. The committees reach consensus regarding the appropriateness of the questions. Questions judged to be acceptable after the committee review are then pretested and analyzed. Questions that are statistically sound are ready to be selected and assembled into test forms.

The SSAT is Reliable

The SSAT is a highly reliable test. The scaled score reliability is higher than .90 for both the verbal and quantitative sections and is approaching .90 for the reading section, which is considered quite high in the educational field.

The SSAT is a Norm-Referenced Test

A norm-referenced test interprets an individual test-taker's score relative to the distribution of scores for a comparison group, referred to as the *norm group*. The SSAT norm groups consist of all the test takers (same grade/same grade & gender) who have taken the test for the first time on one of the Standard Saturday or Sunday SSAT administrations in the United States and Canada over the past three years.

The SSAT reports percentile ranks, which are referenced to the performance of the norm group. For example, if you are a boy in the 8th grade, and your percentile rank on the March 2013 verbal section is 90%, it means that 90% of all the other 8th grade boys' (who have taken the test for the first time on one of the Standard Saturday or Sunday SSAT administrations in the United States and Canada between 2009 and 2012) scores fall below your scaled score. The same scaled score on the SSAT may have a different percentile rank from year to year, and the SSAT percentile ranks should not be compared to those of other standardized tests because each test is taken by a different group of students.

In contrast, a criterion-referenced test interprets a test taker's performance without reference to the performance of other test takers. For example, your percent correct from a classroom math test is 90% because you answered 90% of the questions correctly. Your score is not referenced to the performance of anyone else in your class.

It is important to remember that the SSAT norm group is a highly competitive group. You are being compared to all the other students (same grade/same grade & gender) who are taking this test for admission into independent schools, some of which are the most selective in the country. Most important to remember is that the SSAT is just one piece of information considered by schools when making admission decisions, and for the vast majority of schools, students with a wide range of SSAT scores are admitted.

The SSAT is a Standardized Test

Although each year several different SSAT forms are utilized, the SSAT is administered and scored in a consistent (or standard) manner. The reported scores or scaled scores are comparable and can be used interchangeably, regardless of which test form students take. A scaled score of 500 on the June 2013 Upper Level verbal section, for example, has the same meaning as the scaled score of 500 from the December 2012 Upper Level verbal section, although the forms are different. This score interchangeability is achieved through a statistical procedure referred to as *score equating*. Score equating is used to adjust for minor form difficulty differences, so that the resulting scores can be compared directly.

Standard also refers to the way in which tests are developed and administered. Regarding test development, a standard process for writing, testing, and analyzing questions—before they ever appear on a live test—is used. Further, SSATB provides precise instructions to be followed by qualified and experienced test administrators from the moment you are admitted to the test center until the time of dismissal. Any deviations from the uniform testing conditions are reported by the test administrator in writing to SSATB. Of course, a student with a disability need may apply for testing accommodations, but the processes and procedures for the test's administration remain the same.

Should I Guess on the SSAT?

The answer is: It depends. You must first understand how the test is scored.

When your test is scored, you will receive one point for each correct answer. You will <u>lose</u> one quarter of a point for each incorrect answer. You will not receive or lose points for questions that are not answered. If you guess, try guessing only when you can eliminate one or more answer choices as wrong.

A few things to keep in mind:

Keep moving. Do not waste time on a question that is hard for you. If you cannot answer it, flag or make a note of it in your test book and go on. Go back to it later if there is time.

Earn as many points as you can on easy questions. You receive one point for each correct answer, no matter how hard or easy the questions are. Do not throw away points on questions you know how to answer through careless errors.

Check your answer sheet. Mark your answers in the correct row on the answer sheet. Be especially careful if you skip questions.

THIS PAGE INTENTIONALLY LEFT BLANK.

Chapter Two: About the Upper Level SSAT

The SSAT is a multiple-choice test that consists of verbal, quantitative (math), and reading comprehension sections. The Upper Level SSAT is for students in grades 8-11, and provides admission officers with an idea of your academic ability and "fit" in their schools. The best way to ensure that you perform as well as you possibly can on the SSAT is to familiarize yourself with the test. Familiarity with the format of the test and review of practice questions will make your test-taking experience easier. You'll feel more comfortable with the test and be able to anticipate the types of questions you'll encounter.

This chapter will introduce you to the kinds of questions you'll see on the Upper Level SSAT and the best ways to approach them. The Sample Questions that accompany each section will give you some practice before you tackle the two practice tests that appear later in the book. In this chapter, we also will provide the test-taking strategies that students should know when they take the Upper Level SSAT. The bonus of these test-taking strategies is that they can also help you perform better on the tests you take in school!

> The best way to make sure you perform as well as you can on the SSAT is to become familiar with the test.

The Upper Level Test Consists of FIVE Sections:

1. A Writing Sample

Number of questions: You will have a choice between two prompts.

What it measures: While not scored, this gives admission officers a feel for how well you write and organize your ideas.

Scored section: No, but it is forwarded to the schools you have selected to receive your score reports.

Time allotted: 25 minutes

Topics covered: Students are given a choice between two prompts: one creative writing prompt and one essay-type prompt.

2. A Quantitative (Math) Section

Number of questions: 50, divided into two parts

What it measures: Your ability to solve problems involving arithmetic, elementary algebra, geometry, and other concepts

Scored section: Yes.

Time allotted: 30 minutes for the first 25 questions, and 30 minutes for the final 25 questions

Topics covered:

Number Concepts and Operations

- Arithmetic word problems (including percent, ratio)
- Basic concepts of addition, subtraction, multiplication, and division
- Estimation
- Rational numbers
- Sequences and series
- Frequencies

Algebra (Elementary Concepts)

- Properties of exponents
- Algebraic word problems
- Equations of lines
- Patterns
- Absolute value

Geometry/Measurement

- Area and circumference of a circle
- Area and perimeter of a polygon
- Volume of a cube, cylinder, box
- Pythagorean theory and properties of right, isosceles, and equilateral triangles
- Properties of parallel and perpendicular lines
- Coordinate geometry
- Slope

Data Analysis/Probability

- Interpretation (tables, graphs)
- Trends and inferences
- Probability

3. A Reading Comprehension Section

Number of questions: 40

What it measures: Your ability to read and comprehend

Scored section: Yes.

Time allotted: 40 minutes

Topics covered:

Reading passages generally range in length from 250 to 350 words and may be taken from the following:

- Literary fiction
- Humanities (biography, art, poetry)
- Science (anthropology, astronomy, medicine)
- Social studies (history, sociology, economics)

Questions related to the passage may ask you to:

- Recognize the main idea
- Locate details
- Make inferences
- Derive the meaning of a word or phrase from its context
- Determine the author's purpose
- Determine the author's attitude and tone
- Understand and evaluate opinions/arguments
- Make predictions based on information in the passage

4. A Verbal Section

Number of questions: 60 (30 synonyms and 30 analogies)

What it measures: Vocabulary, verbal reasoning, and ability to relate ideas logically

Scored section: Yes.

Time allotted: 30 minutes

Topics covered: This section covers word similarities and relationships through synonyms and analogies.

5. The Experimental Section

Number of questions: 16

What it measures: The SSATB continually tests new questions to make sure they are reliable, suitable, and acceptable for the SSAT. These questions may be used on a future SSAT form.

Scored section: No.

Time allotted: 15 minutes

Topics covered: This section contains six verbal, five reading, and five quantitative questions for you to answer.

Testing accommodation students requiring 1.5x time are not required to complete the experimental section.

Test Overview		
Section	**Number of Questions**	**Time Allotted To Administer Each Section**
Writing Sample	1	25 minutes
Break		5 minutes
Section 1 (Quantitative)	25	30 minutes
Section 2 (Reading)	40	40 minutes
Break		10 minutes
Section 3 (Verbal)	60	30 minutes
Section 4 (Quantitative)	25	30 minutes
Section 5 (Experimental)	16	15 minutes
Totals	**167[1]**	**3 hours, 5 minutes**

[1]*Of the 167 items including the writing sample, 150 questions are scored.*

I. The Writing Sample

At the beginning of the test, you will be asked to write an essay in 25 minutes. You'll have a choice between a creative and an essay prompt. Your writing sample will be sent to the admission officers at the schools to which you're applying to help them assess your writing skills. This section is not scored by SSATB, and a copy of it is not included with the scores that are provided to your family unless you choose to purchase a copy of your writing sample to accompany your online score report.

What are the Directions for the Writing Sample Section of the Test?

Schools would like to get to know you better through an essay or story using one of the topics below. Please select the topic you find most interesting and fill in the circle next to the topic you choose.

How are the Writing Topics Presented?

The Creative Prompts

The creative prompt is designed to spark your imagination and creativity. It will ask you start a story based on a phrase such as:

> **EXAMPLE**
>
> I put my hand in my pocket and pulled out …
>
> *or*
>
> All I wanted was a glass of water.

The Essay Prompts

The essay-type prompt will ask you to think about something academic or describe something about your life.

> **EXAMPLE**
>
> If you were to create a perfect school, what would it be like and why?
>
> *or*
>
> Who is a person from history you would like to get to know and why?

This is a chance for you to showcase the unique way you think and write.

JUST THE FACTS

The Writing Sample

Number of questions:
You will have a choice between two writing prompts

What this measures:
This gives admission officers a feel for how you write

Scored section:
No, but it is forwarded to the schools you have selected to receive your score reports

Time allotted:
25 minutes

Tips for Getting Your Writing Sample Started

Read the topics carefully. Take a few minutes to think about them and choose the one you prefer. Then organize your thoughts before you begin writing (scrap paper for organizing your thoughts will be provided when you test). Be sure that you use a pencil, that your handwriting is legible, and that you stay within the lines and margins. Remember to be yourself and let your imagination soar!

If you want to change what you write, neatly strike through the words you want to eliminate and add the new words so they are legible. Two line-ruled pages will be provided. Don't feel as if you have to fill both pages—just do your best to provide a well-written story or essay.

Practice Writing Samples

This book includes practice writing sample prompts, which can be found at the beginning of the practice tests. Each sample includes directions, a prompt, and an answer sheet similar to the answer sheet you'll receive during the actual test.

> Remember: Your writing sample will not be scored. Schools use the sample to get to know you better through a story you tell or an essay you write.

Writing Sample Test-Taking Strategies

1. While creativity is encouraged, remember that the admission officers in the schools to which you are applying will be reading your writing sample. You want to be sure that your story/essay is appropriate and one that you would not hesitate to turn in for a school assignment.

2. Read both prompts. Take a couple of minutes to think about what you're going to write. You can use your scrap paper to organize your thoughts.

3. Choose a working title for your story/essay. The Upper Level SSAT doesn't require a title, but a working title will help to keep you on track.

4. Get involved in your story/essay. Provide detail, describe emotions, and have fun.

5. Make sure your story/essay has a beginning, a middle, and an end. Be sure to provide plenty of examples and reasoning in your essay.

6. If there's time, check your writing for correct spelling, punctuation, and grammatical errors.

2. The Quantitative Sections

The two quantitative (mathematics) sections of the Upper Level SSAT measure your knowledge of algebra, geometry, and other quantitative concepts. The words used in SSAT problems refer to mathematical operations with which you are already familiar.

What are the Directions for the Quantitative Section on the Test?

Following each problem in this section, there are five suggested answers. Work each problem in your head or in the blank space provided at the right of the page. Then look at the five suggested answers and decide which one is best.

JUST THE FACTS

The Quantitative Section

Number of questions:
50, divided into two parts

What it measures:
Your ability to solve problems involving arithmetic, elementary algebra, geometry, and other concepts

Scored section: Yes

Time allotted:
30 minutes for the first 25 questions and 30 minutes for the final 25 questions

How are the Quantitative Questions Presented?

Many of the questions that appear in the quantitative sections of the Upper Level SSAT are structured in mathematical terms that directly state the operation you need to perform to determine the best answer choice.

EXAMPLE

1. The slope of the line that is perpendicular to $2x + 3y = 6$ is

   (A) $-\frac{3}{2}$

   (B) $-\frac{2}{3}$

   (C) $-\frac{1}{2}$

   (D) $\frac{2}{3}$

   (E) $\frac{3}{2}$

   The correct answer is (E).

Other questions are structured as word problems. A word problem often does not specifically state the mathematical operation or operations that you will need to perform in order to determine the answer. In these problems, your task is to carefully consider how the question is worded and the way the information is presented to determine what operations you will need to perform.

EXAMPLE

2. At a store, the number of bicycles and the number of automobiles in the parking lot are the same. If the number of bicycle wheels plus the number of automobile wheels equals 30, how many bicycles are at the store?
   (A) 4
   (B) 5
   (C) 6
   (D) 7
   (E) 8

   The correct answer is (B).

Quantitative Test-Taking Strategies

1. Read the question/problem carefully.

2. Pace yourself. Try not to spend too much time on one question.

3. Be sure to use the "Use This Space for Figuring" area of your test book to do the scratch work.

4. Always check to see if you have answered the question asked. Circling what's being asked can be helpful, so you don't mistakenly choose the wrong answer.

5. Watch for unit of measure. Be sure you know and understand in what unit of measurement the answer is supposed to be given.

6. Draw graphics. If you find that a problem is complicated, you can draw a graph, diagram—anything that will allow you to understand what the problem is asking.

7. Remember to mark your answers on the answer sheet! If you solve the question in your answer book and do not mark it on your answer sheet, the answer will not be counted.

Sample Questions: Quantitative

On the following pages, you'll find brief overviews of the Upper Level SSAT math question types you'll encounter on the test. Review each Sample Question description and then complete the questions that illustrate the concept.

Sample Questions: Percentages

Following each problem in this section, there are five suggested answers. Work each problem, then look at the five suggested answers and decide which one is best.

Percent (%) means hundredths or number out of 100, so that $\frac{40}{100}$ = 40 percent, and 3 is 75 percent of 4 (because $\frac{3}{4} = \frac{75}{100}$ = 75 percent).

---

1. If a classroom contains 4 boys and 7 girls, approximately what percent of the students are boys?
   - (A) 25%
   - (B) 36%
   - (C) 57%
   - (D) 60%
   - (E) 70%

---

2. Lucy takes five math tests and scores an average of 71%. The teacher decides to delete one of her tests, making her new average 76%. What was Lucy's grade on the deleted test?
   - (A) 25%
   - (B) 39%
   - (C) 51%
   - (D) 54%
   - (E) 60%

---

3. 18 is what percent of 60?
   - (A) 0.30%
   - (B) 10.8%
   - (C) 18%
   - (D) 30.0%
   - (E) 33.3%

Answer Key: Percentages

1. **Answer (B) 36%**

   Total students = 4 + 7 = 11

   $$\frac{part}{whole} = \frac{percent}{100}$$

   $$\frac{4}{11} = \frac{x}{100}$$

   $x = 36.36 \approx 36\%$

2. **Answer (C) 51%**

   $$\frac{(5 \times 71) - x}{4} = 76$$

   $355 - x = 304$

   $x = 51$

3. **Answer (D) 30.0%**

   $$\frac{part}{whole} = \frac{percent}{100}$$

   $$\frac{18}{60} = \frac{x}{100}$$

   $x = 30\%$

Sample Questions: Fractions

A **fraction** has a numerator and a denominator. The numerator is on top and the denominator is on the bottom. The numerator is divided by the denominator.

For example: $\dfrac{1}{2}$ ↔ numerator ↔ denominator

When fractions have the same numerator but different denominators, the one with the larger denominator is smaller.

For example: $\dfrac{1}{8} < \dfrac{1}{4}$

1. Identify the fraction that is less than $\dfrac{1}{3}$.

   (A) $\dfrac{4}{9}$

   (B) $\dfrac{3}{7}$

   (C) $\dfrac{5}{12}$

   (D) $\dfrac{7}{24}$

   (E) $\dfrac{10}{27}$

2. $\dfrac{2}{3}$ of $\dfrac{1}{2}$ is what fraction?

   (A) $\dfrac{1}{3}$

   (B) $\dfrac{2}{5}$

   (C) $\dfrac{3}{5}$

   (D) $\dfrac{4}{3}$

   (E) $\dfrac{3}{2}$

3. Evaluate $\dfrac{1}{2} + \dfrac{1}{3} + \dfrac{1}{4} + \dfrac{1}{5} =$

   (A) $\dfrac{1}{14}$

   (B) $\dfrac{1}{15}$

   (C) $\dfrac{1}{60}$

   (D) $\dfrac{4}{60}$

   (E) $\dfrac{77}{60}$

Answer Key: Fractions

1. **Answer (D)** $\frac{7}{24}$

   $\frac{1}{3} = \frac{8}{24}$; $\frac{7}{24} < \frac{8}{24}$

2. **Answer (A)** $\frac{1}{3}$

   $\frac{2}{3} \cdot \frac{1}{2} = \frac{1}{3}$

3. **Answer (E)** $\frac{77}{60}$

   The least common denominator is $4 \times 3 \times 5 = 60$.

   $\frac{30}{60} + \frac{20}{60} + \frac{15}{60} + \frac{12}{60} = \frac{77}{60}$

Sample Questions: Decimals

A **decimal point**, which is placed after a whole number, separates the whole-number part from the fractional part of a number. Digits can be placed to the left of the decimal point to indicate values greater than one or to the right of the decimal point to indicate values less than one.

Example: thirty-five and six-tenths written as a decimal number is 35.6

35.6 has 3 tens, 5 ones and 6 tenths

$35.6 = 30 + 5 + \frac{6}{10}$

1. Which number represents one thousand four hundred and thirteen thousandths?
   (A) 1,400.13
   (B) 1,400.013
   (C) 1,400.0013
   (D) 10,400.13
   (E) 100,400.13

2. Divide 191.632 by 8.26
   (A) 23.2
   (B) 23.875
   (C) 24
   (D) 24.2
   (E) 24.401

3. Each of Sean's marbles weighs 0.057 kilograms. A bag containing 12 of the marbles weighs 0.78 kilograms. How many kilograms does the bag weigh by itself?
   (A) 0.057
   (B) 0.096
   (C) 0.684
   (D) 0.711
   (E) 0.723

4. 661.2 + 79.4 + 37.3 + 122.1 =
   (A) 700
   (B) 750
   (C) 800
   (D) 850
   (E) 900

Answer Key: Decimals

1. **Answer (B) 1,400.013**

   $1,400.013 = 1,000 + 400 + \frac{13}{1000}$

2. **Answer (A) 23.2**

   Slide the decimal point two places to the right in both the dividend and in the divisor to create the problem:
   $19163.2 \div 826 = 23.2$

3. **Answer (B) 0.096**

   = total weight minus the weight of the marbles
   = $0.78 - (12 \times 0.057)$
   = 0.096

4. **Answer (E) 900**

   661.2
   79.4
   + 37.3
   122.1
   900.0

Sample Questions: Ratios

A **ratio** compares one quantity with another. When two numbers are compared by division, the indicated division is called a ratio. When two ratios are equal, they form a proportion. A ratio can be expressed in several ways. For example, the ratio 5 to 10 can be expressed as:

$$\frac{5}{10} \qquad 5 \div 10 \qquad 5{:}10$$

1. Joan picked 16 pears, 8 peaches, 6 plums, 2 apples, and 4 bananas at the grocery. What was her ratio of plums to all fruit purchased?
   (A) 6:26
   (B) 6:30
   (C) 1:6
   (D) 3:17
   (E) 1:5

2. Find the ratio of 1 ft. 4 in. to 1 yd.
   (A) 1:2
   (B) 1:3
   (C) 2:5
   (D) 4:5
   (E) 4:9

3. The basketball team won 20 games out of 45 games played. Find the ratio of games won to games lost.
   (A) $\frac{9}{4}$
   (B) $\frac{4}{5}$
   (C) $\frac{2}{3}$
   (D) $\frac{20}{25}$
   (E) $\frac{4}{9}$

Answer Key: Ratios

1. **Answer (C)** 1:6
   The total number of pieces of fruit = 16 + 8 + 6 + 2 + 4 = 36
   The ratio of plums to total = $\frac{6}{36} = \frac{1}{6}$ = 1:6

2. **Answer (E)** 4:9
   1 ft. 4 in. = 16 in.
   1 yd. = 36 in.
   $\frac{16}{36} = \frac{4}{9}$ or 4:9

3. **Answer (B)** $\frac{4}{5}$
   The basketball team won 20 games and lost 25.
   $\frac{20}{25} = \frac{4}{5}$

Sample Questions: Ordering of Numbers

> The symbol > means "greater than." For example, 6 > 4 can be read as "six is greater than four."
> The symbol < means "less than." 6x < 20 can be read "six times some number is less than twenty."

1. If $x < 7$ and $x > -2$, which is a possible solution for x?
   - (A) −4
   - (B) −2
   - (C) 0
   - (D) 7
   - (E) 8

2. Which of the following values is greater than 2.37?
   - (A) 2.28
   - (B) 2.09
   - (C) 2.41
   - (D) 2.17
   - (E) 2.30

Answer Key: Ordering of Numbers

1. **Answer (C) 0**

   $-2 < x < 7$
   Zero is between −2 and 7.

2. **Answer (C) 2.41**

   $$\left(2 + \frac{41}{100}\right) > \left(2 + \frac{37}{100}\right)$$

   $\therefore 2.41 > 2.37$

Sample Questions: Positive and Negative Numbers

> The whole numbers (0, 1, 2, 3...), together with their opposites (0, −1, −2, −3...), are called integers. The counting numbers (1, 2, 3...) are **positive** integers and are sometimes represented by the symbols +1, +2, +3... The numbers −1, −2, −3... are **negative** integers. The number 0 is neither positive nor negative. When two negative numbers are multiplied, the result is a positive integer.

1. Evaluate: -3^2

   (A) −9

   (B) −6

   (C) 3

   (D) 6

   (E) 9

2. $-4(-3)^2 =$

   (A) −24

   (B) −36

   (C) 36

   (D) 144

   (E) −144

3. By what number would you multiply both sides to solve the equation $\frac{x}{5} = -10$?

   (A) −50

   (B) −10

   (C) −5

   (D) 5

   (E) 10

Answer Key: Positive and Negative Numbers

1. **Answer (A) −9**

   $-3^2 = -9$

2. **Answer (B) −36**

   $-4 \times 9 = -36$

3. **Answer (D) 5**

   Multiplication by 5 is the inverse operation of division by 5.

   $\frac{x}{5} = -10$

   $\frac{5}{1} \cdot \frac{x}{5} = -10 \cdot 5$

   $x = -50$

Sample Questions: Sequences

Sequences are number sets that follow a rule that places the numbers in a definite order. For example, "1, 3, 5, 7, 9" is a sequence that results from adding 2 to the first number to get the next number, then adding 2 to that number, and so on. Sequences can follow many patterns. The patterns are the result of the rule.

1. Write the following fractions in the correct increasing sequence:
    $\frac{5}{12}, \frac{3}{8}, \frac{2}{3}$

    (A) $\frac{3}{8}, \frac{2}{3}, \frac{5}{12}$

    (B) $\frac{3}{8}, \frac{5}{12}, \frac{2}{3}$

    (C) $\frac{2}{3}, \frac{5}{12}, \frac{3}{8}$

    (D) $\frac{2}{3}, \frac{3}{8}, \frac{5}{12}$

    (E) $\frac{5}{12}, \frac{2}{3}, \frac{3}{8}$

2. Find the missing number in the sequence:
    ___, 29, 35, 41, 47
    (A) 22
    (B) 23
    (C) 24
    (D) 25
    (E) 26

3. Calculate the fifth term in the sequence that begins:
    $1; \frac{3}{4}; \frac{1}{2}; \frac{1}{4};$ ___

    (A) $\frac{1}{8}$

    (B) $\frac{1}{16}$

    (C) 0

    (D) $-\frac{1}{8}$

    (E) $-\frac{1}{4}$

Answer Key: Sequences

1. **Answer (B)** $\frac{3}{8}, \frac{5}{12}, \frac{2}{3}$

   The least common denominator is 24.

   $\frac{5}{12} = \frac{10}{24}$; $\frac{3}{8} = \frac{9}{24}$; $\frac{2}{3} = \frac{16}{24}$

   $\frac{9}{24} < \frac{10}{24} < \frac{16}{24}$

   $\frac{3}{8} < \frac{5}{12} < \frac{2}{3}$

2. **Answer (B) 23**

   This is an arithmetic sequence in which 6 is added to get each successive term. The first term must be 29 minus 6 = 23.

3. **Answer (C) 0**

   This is an arithmetic sequence in which each successive term is formed by adding $-\frac{1}{4}$. The fifth term is $\frac{1}{4} + \left(-\frac{1}{4}\right) = 0$

Sample Questions: Frequency

When items in a group share at least one characteristic or attribute, the total number of those similar items is called their **frequency**. For example, if the face of a clock has a dot at five-minute intervals, the frequency of those dots is <u>twelve</u> per clock ($60 \div 5 = 12$).

1. You survey 50 people and ask them what kind of telephone they have. Thirty-eight respond that they have a landline phone and 42 have a cell phone. Assuming that each person has at least one telephone, how many have both types of telephones?
   (A) 8
   (B) 30
   (C) 38
   (D) 42
   (E) 80

2. If trains arrive at the train station with a frequency of one every 5 minutes, what is the frequency of arrivals every hour?
   (A) 5
   (B) 12
   (C) 48
   (D) 150
   (E) 300

Answer Key: Frequency

1. **Answer (B) 30**
   $(38 + 42) - 50 = 80 - 50 = 30$

2. **Answer (B) 12**
   $$\frac{1 \text{ train}}{5 \text{ min.}} = \frac{x \text{ trains}}{60 \text{ min.}}$$
   $60 = 5x$
   $12 = x$

Sample Questions: Algebra

Algebra uses numbers, symbols, and letter symbols to solve problems. The basic concept is that one side of the equal sign "=" is, in total, the same as the other. Another important item is the symbol ( ), which indicates that you make the calculations within the symbol (parentheses) before you make those outside the symbol.

In algebra, a letter is used to represent an unknown number until the value of that number is discovered. For example, when 5 is added to some unknown number, the sum is 14 and may be written as follows:

$$5 + n = 14$$

1. If $4x - 3x + 2x = 4 - 3 + 2$, then x equals
   (A) −1
   (B) 0
   (C) 1
   (D) 2
   (E) 3

2. Use the number line below for the following question:
   $\frac{8}{3}$ falls between which of the following 2 numbers?

   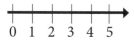

   (A) 0 and 1
   (B) 1 and 2
   (C) 2 and 3
   (D) 3 and 4
   (E) 4 and 5

3. Solve the equation: $13 + x - 2 = 2x$
   (A) 5
   (B) 9
   (C) 11
   (D) 13
   (E) 15

4. Evaluate the expression: $100 - 60(5) + 40 \div 2$
   (A) −180
   (B) −120
   (C) −80
   (D) 120
   (E) 220

Answer Key: Algebra

1. **Answer (C) 1**

   $3x = 3$

   $x = 1$

2. **Answer (C) 2 and 3**

   $\frac{8}{3} = 2\frac{2}{3}$, which is between 2 and 3

3. **Answer (C) 11**

   $11 + x = 2x$

   $11 = x$

4. **Answer (A) –180**

   $100 - 300 + 40 \div 2$

   $= 100 - 300 + 20$

   $= -200 + 20$

   $= -180$

Sample Questions: Geometry and Measurement

Perimeter refers to the distance around the outer boundary of a figure. **Area** refers to the measure of a surface. **Volume** refers to the three-dimensional measure of a shape.

For example, the perimeter of this square is 5 + 5 + 5 + 5 = 20 units.

The area is 5 × 5 = 25 square units.

1. A circle is inscribed inside a square of side length 10. Find the area of the shaded region.

   (A) 10π
   (B) 25
   (C) $100 - 25\pi$
   (D) 25π
   (E) 100

2. The slope of the line that is perpendicular to
   $2x + 3y = 6$ is

   (A) $-\frac{3}{2}$
   (B) $-\frac{2}{3}$
   (C) $-\frac{1}{2}$
   (D) $\frac{2}{3}$
   (E) $\frac{3}{2}$

3. The width of a rectangle is five times its length. If the area of the rectangle is 45, then what is the perimeter of the rectangle?

   (A) 3
   (B) 9
   (C) 15
   (D) 18
   (E) 36

4. A regular polygon has perimeter 110 cm and each side has length 11 cm. How many sides does this polygon have?

   (A) 8
   (B) 9
   (C) 10
   (D) 11
   (E) 12

31

Answer Key: Geometry and Measurement

1. **Answer (C)** $100 - 25\pi$

   = area of square minus area of circle

   $= 10^2 - \pi \times 5^2$

   $= 100 - 25\pi$

2. **Answer (E)** $\frac{3}{2}$

   Given $ax + by = c$, $m = \frac{-a}{b}$

   $\therefore m = \frac{-2}{3}$

   The perpendicular slope is the opposite, reciprocal slope.

   $\therefore m = \frac{3}{2}$

3. **Answer (E)** 36

   Let x = length; $5x$ = width

   $5x^2 = 45$

   $x^2 = 9$

   Then, $x = 3$

   $5x = 15$

   perimeter = 3 + 15 + 3 + 15 = 36

4. **Answer (C)** 10

   Regular polygons have sides of equal lengths.

   $110 \div 11 = 10$ *sides*

Sample Questions: Angle Measurement

Angles are measured in degrees. Degrees are represented by the symbol °. For example, 45 degrees is expressed 45°. A circle contains 360°. The angles that make up a triangle equal 180°. A square or rectangle is made up of four 90° angles, for a total of 360°. The sum of angles that together form a straight line equals 180°.

1. An equilateral triangle has side length 6. Find the perimeter of the triangle.
   - (A) 6
   - (B) 12
   - (C) 18
   - (D) 24
   - (E) 36

2. In the isosceles triangle shown, find the measure of angle B.
   - (A) 32°
   - (B) 60°
   - (C) 58°
   - (D) 74°
   - (E) 148°

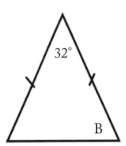

3. The sum of the measures of all the angles of a trapezoid equals
   - (A) 90°
   - (B) 180°
   - (C) 270°
   - (D) 360°
   - (E) 540°

4.

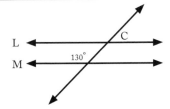

   In the figure, line L is parallel to line M. Find the measure of angle C.
   - (A) 20°
   - (B) 30°
   - (C) 50°
   - (D) 130°
   - (E) 230°

Answer Key: Angle Measurement

1. **Answer (C) 18**

   In an equilateral triangle, all sides are of equal length.

   $\therefore 6 \times 3 = 18$

2. **Answer (D) 74°**

   In an isosceles triangle, the base angles are congruent.

   $\therefore 2B + 32 = 180$

   $2B = 148$

   $B = 74$

3. **Answer (D) 360°**

   A trapezoid is a quadrilateral, or a four-sided polygon.

   Total degrees in a polygon = (number of sides minus 2) times 180.

   $(4 - 2) \times 180$

   $= 360°$

4. **Answer (C) 50°**

   Let X be the angle adjacent to C along the horizontal line.

   Angle X and 130 are supplementary.

   $\therefore$ angle $X = 180° - 130° = 50°$

   Since angle X and angle C are corresponding angles, angle C equals 50°.

Sample Questions: Interpretation of Graphs

Graphs are used to present numerical information in visual form. A **bar graph** (A) is an easy way to compare quantities. A **line graph** (B) is used to record numerical changes over time. A **circle graph** (C) is used when a quantity is divisible into parts and we want to compare the parts.

(A)   (B)   (C)

1. The graph shows the population of Hollyfield from 1983 through 2013. By how many people did the population increase between 1993 and 2003?

    (A) 1,000
    (B) 1,500
    (C) 2,000
    (D) 2,500
    (E) 3,000

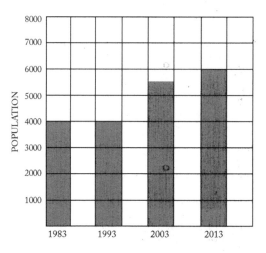

2. The graph shows Daniel's monthly budget while at school. What percentage of his budget is allocated for food and music?

    (A) 21%
    (B) 11%
    (C) 31%
    (D) 44%
    (E) 45%

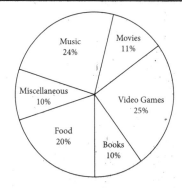

Answer Key: Interpretation of Graphs

1. **Answer (B) 1,500**
    In 2003, the population was approximately 5,500 people.
    In 1993, it was approximately 4,000 people.
    5,500 – 4,000 = 1,500 people.

2. **Answer (D) 44%**
    Music accounts for 24%. Food accounts for 20%. Together they account for
    24% + 20% = 44%.

3. The Reading Comprehension Section

By presenting passages and questions about the passages, the Reading Comprehension section measures your ability to understand what you read. After you read each passage, you'll be asked questions about its content or about the author's style, intent, or point of view. In general, the SSAT uses two types of writing: **narrative**, which includes excerpts from novels, poems, short stories, or essays; and **argument**, which presents a definite point of view about a subject. The passages are chosen from a variety of categories, including but not limited to:

- **Humanities**: art, biography, poetry, etc.
- **Social Studies**: history, economics, sociology, etc.
- **Science**: medicine, astronomy, zoology, etc.

JUST THE FACTS

Reading Comprehension

Number of questions:
40

What it measures:
Your ability to read and comprehend what you read

Scored section:
Yes

Time allotted:
40 minutes

What are the Directions for the Reading Comprehension Section on the Test?

Read each passage carefully and then answer the questions about it. For each question, decide on the basis of the passage which one of the choices best answers the question.

What Types of Questions are Presented in the Reading Comprehension Section?

Most of the questions in the reading comprehension section focus on the following:

1. **Determining the main idea**

    Selecting the main idea in the passage
    Examples:
    - Which of the following best states the main idea of the passage?
    - The passage is primarily about…

    Choosing the best title for the passage
    Examples:
    - Which of the following is the best title for the selection?
    - The headline that best fits the article is…

2. Locating details

Understanding specific references or a section in the passage
Examples:
- According to the passage, what happens when the bell rings?
- In the first paragraph, the writer describes…

Identifying specific things about the passage
Examples:
- The "beginning" (line 15) probably refers to…
- According to the author, who was Nelly visiting?

Determining key terms used in the passage
Examples:
- As used in the sentence, "justification" (line 5) most nearly means
- In line 13, the word "relinquish" means…

3. Drawing inferences

Fitting together ideas in the passage to determine their relationships
Examples:
- In the poem, the "rain," "sand," and "heat" (lines 1-3) suggest that…
- It can be inferred from the passage that the location of the event is most likely…

Assuming things about the passage even though they may not be stated directly
Examples:
- The water disappeared most likely because…
- "The rock is transformed" (line 25) probably means…

4. Identifying tone or mood

Determining the tone, mood, or style of the passage
Examples:
- The critic's tone can best be described as which of the following?
- The writer's style is best described as…

How are the Reading Comprehension Questions Presented?

The SSAT presents each passage (or poem) with a corresponding group of three to six questions. The directions instruct you to read each passage and answer the questions about it.

> We had a consuming desire to see a pony rider, but somehow or other all that passed us streaked by in the night, and so we heard only a whiz and a hail, and the swift phantom was gone. But now the driver exclaims: "Here he comes!" Every neck is stretched and every eye strained.
>
> Line 5
>
> Away across the endless dead level of the prairie a black speck appears. Soon it becomes a horse and rider, rising and falling, sweeping nearer and nearer, and the flutter of hoofs comes faintly to the ear. Another instant a whoop and hurrah from our upper deck, a wave of the rider's hand, but no reply, and man and horse burst past our excited faces and go winging away like a belated fragment of a storm!

1. At the driver's call, the people became more
   - (A) eager
   - (B) puzzled
   - (C) hysterical
   - (D) frightened
   - (E) disappointed

The correct answer is (A), eager, as shown by the sentence "Every neck is stretched and every eye strained" in response to the driver's call. The other answer choices give possible reactions to the exclamation, but none of them corresponds to the author's description of the people.

2. Which of the following can you infer from the passage?
   - (A) The pony rider was traveling in the same direction as the author.
   - (B) The pony rider was unable to speak.
   - (C) The writer traveled at night.
   - (D) The author was on the upper deck when the pony rider passed.
   - (E) The pony rider was a phantom.

The correct answer is (C), the writer traveled at night. The author refers to "all that passed us streaked by in the night."

3. This passage can best be described as
   - (A) an account of an event
   - (B) a news article
   - (C) a research study
   - (D) an epic poem
   - (E) an advertisement

The correct answer is (A), an account of an event. The passage is more descriptive and subjective than a typical news article or research study. There is no similarity to an epic poem, and the passage does not promote a product or service.

How Do You Answer the Reading Comprehension Questions?

As you read, determine the main idea of the passage or poem. Identify the important details that move the narrative along or create a mood or tone. In an argument, identify the details that support the writer's opinion. The first sentence of each paragraph will give you a general sense of the topic. Identify the topic of each paragraph and underline key facts. Try to figure out the writer's intention, or purpose of the passage. Notice the writer's attitude, tone, and general style.

These habits can help you understand what you read, whether you are taking the Upper Level SSAT, preparing for a history test, or getting ready to write an essay for your English class.

Reading Comprehension Test-Taking Strategies

1. Take time to read and understand the first sentence of each paragraph. This will provide you with a general sense of the topic.

2. Scan the answer choices, since they are generally short and provide excellent clues. If an answer choice refers you to a specific line in the passage, underline that line for reference.

3. Read each passage carefully. Follow the author's reasoning. Notice attitude, tone, and general style.

4. Pay attention to words such as always, never, every, and none. They may play an important role in the answer.

5. Identify the topic of each paragraph, key facts, and the author's purpose for writing. Underline the key facts for quick reference.

6. Remember to read for the characteristics of the passage, not for information or to acquire an understanding of the topic.

7. Read all answer choices carefully before you choose. When you find an answer choice that fails to satisfy the requirements of the question and statement, cross it out.

Sample Questions: Reading Comprehension

Directions: Read each passage carefully and then answer the questions about it. For each question, decide on the basis of the passage which one of the choices best answers the question.

We had been five days in the hunting camp, and the meat, which had all this time been drying in the sun, was now fit for transportation. Sufficient buffalo hides also had been obtained to make the next season's lodges; but it remained to provide the long poles on which they were to be supported. These were only to be had among the

Line 5   tall spruce woods in the hills, and in that direction, therefore, our next move was to be made. Amid the general abundance of the camp at this time, there were no instances of individual want; for, although the hide and tongue of the buffalo belong by exclusive right to the hunter who has killed it, anyone else is equally entitled to help himself from the rest of the carcass. Thus the weak, the aged, and even the lazy come in for a share of

10   the spoils, and many a helpless old woman, who would otherwise perish from starvation, is sustained in abundance.

---

1. The main reason for staying five days in the hunting camp was to
   (A) allow the meat to dry
   (B) obtain spruce poles
   (C) secure additional buffalo hides
   (D) provide for the aged and helpless
   (E) eat as much of the fresh meat as possible

2. The hunter who killed a buffalo
   (A) was entitled to the better cuts of meat
   (B) could do anything he wished with the carcass
   (C) shared the carcass only with his elderly relatives
   (D) could take only the hide and tongue before sharing the carcass
   (E) usually gave the carcass to the old and infirm and to the sick

3. According to the passage, the buffalo hides were to be used in making
   (A) canoes
   (B) clothing
   (C) blankets
   (D) dwellings
   (E) moccasins

4. Which of the following conclusions can best be drawn from the passage?
   (A) There was no permanent settlement and the entire tribe was at the hunting camp.
   (B) There was no permanent settlement, but there were several separate camps that moved along together.
   (C) There was no permanent settlement and the entire tribe, with the exception of the weak and the aged, was at the hunting camp.
   (D) While the hunters were at the hunting camp, the rest of the tribe remained in a permanent settlement up in the hills.
   (E) While the hunters were at the hunting camp, the rest of the tribe remained at a permanent settlement at a location not given.

Praise is the reflection of virtue; but it is as the glass or body which giveth the reflection. If it be from the common people, it is commonly false and naught; and rather followeth vain persons than virtuous. For the common people understand not many excellent virtues. The lowest virtues draw praise from them; the middle virtues work
Line 5 in them astonishment or admiration; but of the highest virtues they have no sense of perceiving at all. Certainly fame is like a river, that beareth up things light and swollen, and drowns things weighty and solid. But if persons of quality and judgment concur, then it is a good name like unto a sweet ointment. It filleth all round about, and will not easily away. There be so many false points of praise, that a man may justly hold it a
10 suspect.

Some praises come of good wishes and respects, which is a form due in civility to kings and great persons, to teach in praising, when by telling men what they are, they represent to them what they should be.

Some men are praised maliciously to their hurt, thereby to stir envy and jealousy
15 towards them: The worst kind of enemies are they that praise. Certainly moderate praise, used with opportunity, and not vulgar, is that which doth the good. Too much magnifying of man or matter doth irritate contradiction, and procure envy and scorn. To praise a man's self cannot be decent, except it be in rare cases; but to praise a man's office or profession, he may do it with good grace, and with a kind of magnanimity.

5. The author refers to praise as "the glass or body which giveth the reflection" (lines 1-2). Which statement best captures the author's meaning?

(A) Praise is transparent, much like glass.

(B) People praise only people they understand.

(C) One should look at oneself before judging others.

(D) Praise is more reflective of the giver than the receiver.

(E) Praise reflects one's feeling similar to the way glass reflects light.

6. In the context of the passage, the word "vulgar" (line 16) means

(A) spiteful

(B) common

(C) rewarding

(D) attractive

(E) opportune

7. The main point made by the passage is that

(A) praise is good for us

(B) praise has but one purpose

(C) praise is often undeserved

(D) some people praise anything

(E) praise shouldn't be taken at face value

8. The attitude of the author toward "the common people" (line 3) is one of

(A) envy

(B) respect

(C) curiosity

(D) contempt

(E) amusement

Answer Key: Reading Comprehension

1.   **(A)** The passage states that they stayed "five days in the hunting camp to allow the meat to dry" (lines 1-2).

2.   **(D)** The passage states that "although the hide and tongue of the buffalo belong by exclusive right to the hunter who has killed it, anyone else is equally entitled to help himself from the rest of the carcass."

3.   **(D)** The statement that "Sufficient buffalo hides also had been obtained to make the next season's lodges" means the hides would be used to build places to live in.

4.   **(A)** It can be inferred from the passage that the tribe did not have a permanent settlement "because the weak, the aged, and even the lazy" were present at the hunting camp.

5.   **(D)** It can be inferred from the first sentence that praise is more characteristic of one who gives it rather than one who receives it.

6.   **(B)** In the context of the passage, it can be inferred that vulgar means common.

7.   **(E)** The main idea of the passage is to be skeptical when receiving praise because that praise may be more characteristic of the giver than of the receiver.

8.   **(D)** The author's attitude in line 3 is best described as contempt because he suggests that praise given by common people is lacking substance or worth.

4. The Verbal Section

The Verbal section of the Upper Level SSAT asks you to identify **synonyms** and to interpret **analogies**. The synonym questions test the strength of your vocabulary. The analogy questions measure your ability to relate ideas to each other logically.

Synonyms

Synonyms are words that have the same or nearly the same meaning as another word. For example, *fortunate* is a synonym for *lucky*; *tidy* is a synonym for *neat*; and *difficult* is a synonym for *hard*. Synonym questions on the SSAT ask you to choose a word that has a meaning similar to that of a given word.

What are the Directions for the Synonym Section on the Test?

Each of the following questions consists of one word followed by five words or phrases. You are to select the one word or phrase whose meaning is closest to that of the word in capital letters.

How are the Synonym Questions Presented?

The Upper Level SSAT presents vocabulary questions as a single word in capital letters, and your task is to choose the word that is most similar in meaning to the word in capital letters.

> EXAMPLE
>
> 1. INCOGNITO:
>   (A) lost
>   (B) replaced
>   (C) concealed
>   (D) uncovered
>   (E) distinguished
>   **The correct answer is (C), concealed.**

> EXAMPLE
>
> 2. CONDESCEND:
>   (A) patronize
>   (B) deceive
>   (C) censor
>   (D) remove
>   (E) specialize
>   **The correct answer is (A), patronize.**

> EXAMPLE
>
> 3. LACKLUSTER:
>   (A) harsh
>   (B) smug
>   (C) soggy
>   (D) parched
>   (E) dull
>   **The correct answer is (E), dull.**

JUST THE FACTS

The Verbal Section

Number of questions: 60 (30 synonyms and 30 analogies)

What it measures: Vocabulary, verbal reasoning, and ability to relate ideas logically

Scored section: Yes

Time allotted: 30 minutes

How Do You Answer Synonym Questions?

There is only one correct response, so make sure you read the question carefully. There are no context clues in the Upper Level SSAT vocabulary format. If the word tested is unfamiliar to you, you could use the process of elimination to choose the correct answer. In other words, eliminate or cross out any of the words that you know are not the correct answer. In this way, you can narrow down your choices.

How Can You Build Your Vocabulary?

The best way to prepare is to read as much as you can to build your vocabulary. If you encounter an unfamiliar word in your reading, make sure you look it up in a dictionary (either online or in print). Keep track of the word and its meaning on an index card, notepad, or in your notes on your smartphone. Keeping track of new words or words that are unfamiliar to you will help you build a tremendous vocabulary.

Another way to prepare is to learn the meaning of the word parts that make up many English words. These word parts consist of **prefixes, suffixes,** and **roots**. If you encounter an unfamiliar word, you could take apart the word and think about the parts.

> The greater your vocabulary, the greater your chance of getting the correct answer.

Prefixes

Prefix	Meaning	Example
a-, an-	not, without, opposite to	antonym
ab-	from	absent
ad-	to, toward	advance
ante-	before	anteroom
anti-	against, opposite	antibacterial
auto-	self	autobiography
bi-	two	bicycle
circum-	around	circumference
de-	away from	depart
dia-	through, across	diagonal
dis-	away from, not	disappear, disloyal
en-	put in, into	enter
ex-	out of, former	exit, exasperation
extra-	outside of, beyond	extraordinary
hyper-	over, more	hyperactive
il-, ir-	not, without	illuminate, irritate
in-, im-	into, not	insert, impossible
inter-	between	interact
intra-	within	intrastate
macro-	large	macroeconomics
mal-	bad, wrong	malady, malpractice
micro-	small	microscope
mono-	one	monopoly, monotonous
multi-	many	multicolor
non-	without, not	nonsense
peri-	around	perimeter
post-	after	postscript
pre-, pro-	before, forward	preview, prologue
semi- (also hemi-)	half	semicircle, hemisphere
sub-	under	subway, submarine
syn-	same	synonym
trans-	across	transport, transit
tri-	three	tricycle
un-	not	unknowing
uni-	one, together	unity

Suffixes

Suffix	Meaning	Example
-able	able to be	habitable
-acy	state or quality	privacy
-al	act or process of	theatrical
-an (-ian)	relating to, belonging to	American
-ance, -ence	state or quality of	brilliance
-ant	a person who	supplicant
-arian	a person who	librarian
-ate	have or be characterized by	desolate
-cide	act of killing	genocide
-cracy	rule, government, power	aristocracy
-dom	place or state of being	wisdom
-dox	belief	orthodox
-en	become	smarten
-er, -or	one who	lover
-ese	relating to a place	Japanese
-esque	in the style of/like	arabesque, grotesque
-fy /-ify	make, cause (makes the word a verb)	beautify, certify
-ful	full of	graceful
-gam/-gamy	marriage, union	monogamous
-gon/-gonic	angle	decagon
-hood	state, condition, or quality	parenthood
-ile	relating to, capable of	domicile, juvenile
-ious, -ous	characterized by	contagious
-ish	having the quality of	devilish
-ism	doctrine, belief	socialism
-ist	one who	dramatist
-ity, -ty	quality of	ferocity
-ive	having the nature of	talkative
-ize	become	prioritize
-log(ue)	word, speech	analogy, dialogue
-ment	condition of	commitment
-ness	state of being	faithfulness
-phile	one who loves	Francophile
-phobia	abnormal fear of	agoraphobia
-ship	position held	scholarship
-sion, -tion	state of being	abbreviation

Word Roots   G = Greek   L = Latin

Root	Meaning	Example
annu, enni (L)	year	anniversary, perennial
anthrop (G)	man	anthropomorphism
ast(er)(G)	star	astrology, asterisk
audi (L)	hear	audible, audience
auto (G)	self	autobiography
bene (L)	good	beneficial
bio (G)	life	biography, biology
chrono (G)	time	chronology
civ (L)	citizen	civilization, civilian
cred (L)	believe	credential, creed
dem(o) (G)	people	democracy
dict (L)	say	dictation, dictator
duc (L)	lead, make	conduct, deduct
gen (L)	give birth	genesis, generation
geo (G)	earth	geometry
graph (G)	write	dysgraphia, graphic
jur, jus (L)	law	jurisprudence, juror
log, logue (L)	thought, word	logical
luc (L)	light	lucid, translucent
man(u) (L)	hand	manual, manufacture
mand, mend (L)	order	command
min (L)	small	minimal
mis, mit (L)	send	missile, transmit
nov (L)	new	novel
omni (L)	all	omnivore
pan (G)	all	pan-American, panacea
patr (G) pater (L)	father	patriot
path (G)	feel	sympathy
phil (G)	love	philosophy, Philadelphia
phon (G)	sound	phonetic, telephone
photo (G)	light	photosynthesis
poli (G)	city	political, politician
port (L)	carry	deport, report
qui(t) (L)	quiet, rest	tranquility, quiet
scrib, script (L)	write	prescribe
sens, sent (L)	feel	sentiment
sol (L)	sun	solarium

Word Roots   G = Greek   L = Latin

Root	Meaning	Example
tele (G)	far off	television
terr (L)	earth	terrestrial
tract (L)	drag, draw	detract, tractor
vac (L)	empty	evacuation
vid, vis (L)	see	invisible, videographer
vit (L)	life	vitality, vitamin
zo (G)	life	zoology

Sample Questions: Synonyms

Directions: Each of the following questions consists of a word followed by five words or phrases. You are to select the one word or phrase whose meaning is closest to the word in capital letters.

1. TENACIOUS:
   (A) sloppy
   (B) complete
   (C) uncertain
   (D) vulnerable
   (E) holding fast

2. LAMENT:
   (A) shiny
   (B) mourn
   (C) argue
   (D) sickly
   (E) adhere

3. CONNIVE:
   (A) plot
   (B) drop
   (C) trick
   (D) wrinkle
   (E) estimate

4. NOXIOUS:
   (A) fowl
   (B) alarm
   (C) twirl
   (D) toxic
   (E) evening

5. PARADIGM:
   (A) compassion
   (B) centerpiece
   (C) patchwork
   (D) model
   (E) irony

6. LOQUACIOUS:
   (A) reserved
   (B) inarticulate
   (C) essential
   (D) charming
   (E) wordy

7. ACUMEN:
   (A) despair
   (B) charisma
   (C) narcissism
   (D) self-denial
   (E) shrewdness

8. FLAMBOYANT:
   (A) showy
   (B) seemly
   (C) common
   (D) repulsive
   (E) standoffish

Answer Key: Synonyms

1. **(E) holding fast**
2. **(B) mourn**
3. **(A) plot**
4. **(D) toxic**
5. **(D) model**
6. **(E) wordy**
7. **(E) shrewdness**
8. **(A) showy**

Verbal Analogies

An **analogy** is a comparison between two things that are usually seen as different from each other but have some similarities. These types of comparisons play an important role in improving problem-solving and decision-making skills, in perception and memory, in communication and reasoning skills, and in reading and building vocabulary. Analogies help students to process information actively, make important decisions, and improve understanding and long-term memory. Considering these relationships stimulates critical and creative thinking.

> The analogy portion of the SSAT asks you to identify the answer that best matches the relationship between two words.

What are the Directions for the Verbal Analogies Section on the Test?

The following questions ask you to find relationships between words. For each question, select the answer choice that best completes the meaning of the sentence.

What are the Things to Remember When Doing Analogies?

Parts of Speech

If the words in the first pair express a "noun/adjective" or "verb/noun" relationship, for example, the second pair should show the same relationship.

Word Order

If the first pair expresses a particular relationship, the second pair must express the same relationship in the same order.

Exactness

Sometimes two or more of the given choices would make sense. When this happens, choose the answer that most exactly suits the relationship between the words in the question.

How are Verbal Analogies Presented?

The SSAT analogy questions are presented two ways.

Two-part stem—"A" is to "B" as...

In this form, you will be presented with two words in the **stem** (the pair of words or the three words presented in the question) and given the task to select the option that contains the pair of words with the same relationship as the pair of words "A" and "B."

EXAMPLE

1. Meandering is to river as
    (A) winding is to road
    (B) wandering is to wave
    (C) amassing is to cloud
    (D) chugging is to cloud
    (E) rolling is to ship
    The correct answer is (A), winding is to road.

Three-part stem—"A" is to "B" as "C" is to...

Some analogies supply three of the four necessary words. In this form, you will be presented with three words in the stem and your task is to find the relationship between the first two words and then choose a word that is related to the third word in the same way.

> **EXAMPLE**
>
> 2. Clear is to printing as articulate is to
>   (A) painting
>   (B) driving
>   (C) listening
>   (D) speaking
>   (E) walking
>   The correct answer is (D), speaking.

What are Verbal Analogy Relationships?

Some of the most common analogy relationships that you will find on the SSAT include the following:

1. **Synonym Relationships:** Relationships between synonyms, or words that have very similar meaning. **EXAMPLE:** home is to house as car is to vehicle

2. **Antonym Relationships:** Relationships between antonyms—words that are the opposite in meaning, or words that are nearly the opposite in meaning. **EXAMPLE:** fast is to slow as high is to low

3. **Defining Relationships:** Relationships defined by a verb or a verbal relationship. **EXAMPLE:** carpenter is to house as cook is to dinner

4. **Type/Kind Relationships:** Relationships that describe how one word in a pair is a kind or type of the other word. **EXAMPLE:** novel is to book as elm is to tree

5. **Degree Relationships:** Relationships in which one word is related to the other by degree. **EXAMPLE:** hurricane is to gust as downpour is to drizzle

6. **Part/Whole Relationships:** Relationships in which the first word is a part of the second word. **EXAMPLE:** chapter is to book as actor is to ensemble

7. **Whole/Part Relationships:** Relationships in which the second word is a part of the first word. **EXAMPLE:** book is to chapter as ensemble is to actor

8. **Word Relationships:** Relationships that are grammatical. **EXAMPLE:** meet is to met as run is to ran

9. **Noun/Verb Relationships:** Relationships in which one of the words names a place, person, or idea, while the other represents an associated action. **EXAMPLE:** bake is to bread as drive is to automobile

10. **Individual to Object Relationships:** Relationships that involve a person who has or uses an object. **EXAMPLE:** golfer is to clubs as architect is to blueprint

11. **Function Relationships:** Relationships that define the purpose of the words. **EXAMPLE:** chair is to sit as book is to read

12. **Cause-and-Effect Relationships:** Relationships that describe how one word in a pair may produce the other. **EXAMPLE:** cow is to milk as bee is to honey

13. **Purpose Relationships:** Relationships in which one of the words of each pair is used in a task that involves the other word in the pair. **EXAMPLE:** bat is to ball as stick is to puck

14. **Association Relationships:** Relationships in which one word in a pair is perceived as having a connection with the other word. **EXAMPLE:** chicken is to poultry as pig is to pork

Verbal Test-Taking Strategies

1. The best way to improve your vocabulary is to read, read, and read some more.

2. Take note of unfamiliar words and look up their meanings.

3. Review the words you don't know.

4. Practice your vocabulary by taking the practice tests in this book. If you missed any of the verbal questions, read the questions and answers again, so you'll understand why you answered those questions incorrectly. Look them up and write them down.

> If the analogy has a two-part stem, then review the pair of words in each answer choice and establish the relationship between the pair of words in the stem. If the analogy has a three-part stem, then review the answer choices and try to establish the relationship with the third word in the stem.

How Do You Solve Verbal Analogy Questions?

A great strategy for solving analogies is to use the "bridge sentence." Bridge sentences help you quickly recognize the pair of words that make up the answer by "plugging in" the answer pair to the bridge sentence that you created from the stem. If your bridge sentence works with both the stem and the answer pair, you've answered the question correctly.

First, you should try to determine the meaning of the initial pair of words in the stem. Then figure out how the first two words are related. Next, create a bridge sentence that expresses that relationship. Try your sentence using each answer choice. As soon as you determine that an answer choice does not fit, eliminate it as a possible answer and go to the next choice. If you find that there is more than one answer, or that there is no answer, go back to see if a different relationship—a different bridge sentence—fits better. We've provided a list of relationships on the previous page, but remember that the list does not include all of the relationships that you might find on the Upper Level SSAT.

> Be careful of the order of the words when you're determining the corresponding relationships.

Keep in mind that the relationships between the words in analogies can take many forms. They may be opposites, such as *up* and *down*. They may be actions, such as *hop* and *rabbit*. The analogy may even involve combinations of relationships. Think about the words *airplane* and *helicopter*: Each is a vehicle, someone operates each one (a pilot), and each has a particular place in which it operates (the sky). So an analogy for *airplane is to helicopter* might be *automobile is to truck*, because both are vehicles that have drivers and both operate on roads. Another analogy is *yacht is to submarine*, because both are vehicles, both have people who operate them, and both operate in water.

Try thinking of the analogy portion of the SSAT as the brainteaser section. So when you're teasing out the meanings of analogies, don't focus only on the meanings of words. The relationship between the words is as important as their meaning. And the good news about analogies is that you can get better at solving them with practice!

The following analogy examples will give you an idea of how the SSAT analogy questions are presented. Each question corresponds to one of the "relationships" already discussed. Next, you'll get an opportunity to practice in the Sample Questions section that follows.

EXAMPLE

1. Cumbersome is to awkward as
   (A) reasonable is to enormous
   (B) miniature is to tiny
   (C) overdone is to moderate
   (D) objective is to subjective
   (E) skillful is to rambling

The correct answer is (B). This example presents a *synonym* relationship. A synonym for "cumbersome" is "awkward." Something that is cumbersome is awkward. Something that is "miniature" is by definition "tiny."

EXAMPLE

2. Stream is to river as brook is to
   (A) land
   (B) water
   (C) creek
   (D) forest
   (E) puddle

The correct answer is (C). This example presents a relationship of *degree*. A "stream" is smaller than a "river" and a "brook" is smaller than a "creek."

EXAMPLE

3. Sentence is to paragraph as
   (A) dawn is to day
   (B) text is to story
   (C) path is to work
   (D) book is to library
   (E) classroom is to students

The correct answer is (D). This example presents a *part/whole* relationship. A sentence is "part" of a paragraph; sentences form or make up a paragraph. A book is "part" of a library; books make up or form a library.

EXAMPLE

4. Watercolor is to painting as jazz is to
   (A) music
   (B) theme
   (C) artist
   (D) orchestra
   (E) relationship

The correct answer is (A). This example presents a *type/kind* relationship. A watercolor is a particular type of painting and jazz is a particular type of music.

EXAMPLE

5. Epidemic is to disease as
   (A) famine is to hunger
   (B) creative is to creation
   (C) persuasion is to composition
   (D) mountainous is to climb
   (E) ache is to gluttony

The correct answer is (A). This is an example of a *degree* relationship. An epidemic is a widespread outbreak of an infectious disease as famine can be widespread hunger.

Sample Questions: Analogies

Directions: The following questions ask you to find relationships between words. For each question, select the answer choice that best completes the meaning of the sentence.

1. Breeze is to wind as whiff is to
   (A) noise
   (B) odor
   (C) water
   (D) whisper
   (E) laughter

2. Canoe is to boat as
   (A) room is to house
   (B) wheat is to oat
   (C) sedan is to car
   (D) pint is to gallon
   (E) shark is to whale

3. Trim is to budget as
   (A) decorate is to tree
   (B) reduce is to production
   (C) fit is to athlete
   (D) adjust is to recipe
   (E) spill is to fuel

4. Glean is to disburse as
   (A) grain is to plant
   (B) collect is to scatter
   (C) wash is to dirt
   (D) assemble is to construct
   (E) guess is to know

5. Liter is to volume as
   (A) pound is to weight
   (B) kilogram is to meter
   (C) pint is to gallon
   (D) volt is to electricity
   (E) inch is to ruler

6. Mnemonic is to memory as
   (A) paint is to canvas
   (B) belief is to myth
   (C) eyeglasses is to vision
   (D) universe is to telescope
   (E) skyscraper is to architect

7. Pedestrian is to ordinary as furtive is to
   (A) secretive
   (B) trustworthy
   (C) compassionate
   (D) stubborn
   (E) remorseful

8. Satellite is to orbit as
   (A) shuttle is to spacecraft
   (B) ship is to course
   (C) monument is to sculptor
   (D) automobile is to traffic light
   (E) television is to remote

Answer Key: Analogies

1. **(B) odor**
   Wind may be experienced (felt) in the form of slight breeze, just as odor may be experienced (smelled) in the form of a slight whiff.

2. **(C) sedan is to car**
   A canoe is an example of a type of boat, just as a sedan is a type of car.

3. **(B) reduce is to production**
   If a budget is trimmed, it is made smaller; if production is reduced, it is made smaller.

4. **(B) collect is to scatter**
   Glean and disburse are opposing actions, just as collect and scatter are opposing actions.

5. **(A) pound is to weight**
   A liter is a unit of volume, just as a pound is a unit of weight.

6. **(C) eyeglasses is to vision**
   A mnemonic improves your memory, just as eyeglasses improve your vision.

7. **(A) secretive**
   Something that is pedestrian is ordinary or dull; someone who is furtive is secretive.

8. **(B) ship is to course**
   A satellite follows a path called its orbit, just as a ship follows a path called its course.

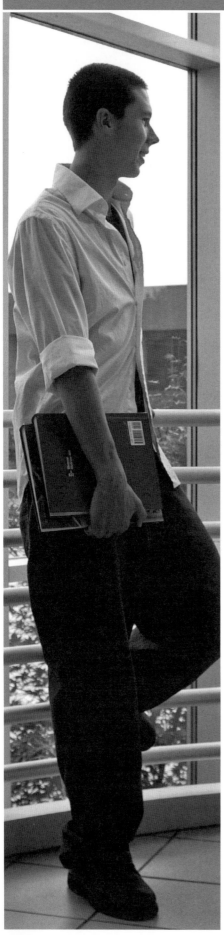

Summing It Up

Here are a few things to keep in mind when you take the Upper Level SSAT:

- Make sure that you understand the directions before you start to work on any section. If there is anything that you do not understand, read the directions again.

- You don't need to answer every question on the test to score well. Some of the questions will be very easy and others will be difficult. Whenever the test is administered, most students find that they do not know the answer to every question in every section. By working as quickly as you can without rushing, you should be able to read and think about every question.

- If you are not sure of an answer to a question, put a question mark (?) in the margin and move on. Make sure you also skip that question's answer bubble on your answer sheet! If you have time, you can come back to questions you have not answered.

- You may make as many marks on the test booklet as you need to. Just be sure to mark your answers on the answer sheet!

- Answers written in the test book will not count toward your score. Space is provided in the book for scratch work in the quantitative sections. Check often to make sure that you are marking your answer in the correct row on the answer sheet.

- If you decide to change an answer, be sure to erase your first mark on the answer sheet completely.

Chapter Three: Scores

What Your Scores Mean

If you're like most people, you'll quickly scan the score report trying to find **the** magic number that will tell you whether the scores are good or bad. With an admission test like the SSAT, this is not an easy thing to do. First, one must remember that the purpose of an admission test is to offer a common measure of academic ability, which can be used to compare all applicants. In the case of the SSAT, the test-taker population is a relatively homogeneous one—students applying to college-preparatory private/independent schools. Given this, it is important to keep in mind that the test taker's scores are being compared only to students in this academically elite group.

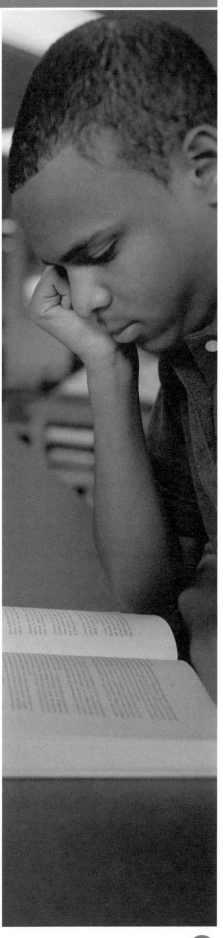

> It's fair to say that the SSAT is difficult because *it is designed to be.*

As described in Chapter 1, admission tests differ from other tests such as classroom and achievement tests in significant ways. Achievement and classroom tests both assess a specific body of knowledge that should have been covered in the class and school year. If all students perform well, the teacher and school system have fulfilled their objective. If all students performed well on an admission test, it would lose its value in helping differentiate between and among candidates. The overall difficulty level of the SSAT is built to be at 50%-60%. Thus, it's fair to say that the SSAT is difficult because *it is designed to be.*

Formula Scoring

The SSAT uses a method of scoring known in the testing industry as "Formula Scoring." Students earn one point for every correct answer, receive no points for omitted questions, and lose ¼ point for each incorrect answer (since each question has 5 choices). This is different from "Right Scoring," which computes the total score by counting the number of correct answers, with no penalty for incorrect answers. Formula scoring is used to make the test taker's expected gain from random guessing equal to zero.

Test takers are instructed to omit questions for which they cannot make an educated guess. Since most students have not encountered this kind of test before, it is an important area for students to understand and in which to have some experience prior to taking the SSAT. SSAT score reports provide detailed information by section on the number of questions right, wrong, and not answered to aid families and schools in understanding the student's test-taking strategy and scores.

What do Admission Officers Consider?

It cannot be said often enough: *admission test scores are only one piece of the application.* The degree of emphasis placed on scores in a school's admission process depends on that school and on other information, such as transcripts, applicants' statements, and teacher recommendations.

The descriptions indicated by the letters below correspond to the lettered sections on the sample score report on page 59.

Ⓐ About You

Review this section carefully. Is the student's name spelled correctly? Is the date of birth listed correctly? And—very important—when registering the student, did you list his/her current grade? The student's current grade is used to determine which test form he/she will take and also dictates the comparison or norm groups (SSAT Percentiles). If you mistakenly list the grade to which your child is applying, he/she may get the wrong form and his/her SSAT Scaled Score will be compared with students a year (or grade) older. If any of this information is incorrect, contact SSATB immediately.

Ⓑ The Test You Took

Again, review this information for accuracy. For Test Level, the student will have taken either the Middle Level SSAT for students in grades 5-7 who are applying to grades 6-8, or the Upper Level SSAT for students in grades 8-11 who are applying to grades 9-12. There is a different score scale for each of these levels.

Ⓒ Your Scaled Scores

SSAT scores are listed by section so you can understand the student's performance on each of the three scored sections: Verbal, Quantitative/Math, and Reading. A total score (a sum of the three sections) is also reported. For the Upper Level SSAT, the lowest number on the scale (500) is the lowest possible score a student can earn, and the highest number (800) is the highest possible score a student can earn.

Scores are first calculated by awarding one point for each correct answer and subtracting one-quarter of one point for each incorrect answer. These scores are called raw scores. Raw scores can vary from one edition of the test to another due to differences in difficulty among different editions. A statistical procedure called "equating" is used to adjust for these differences. After equating, the reported scores or scaled scores (e.g., the scores on the 500-800 scale for the Upper Level test) can be compared to each other across forms.

Personal Score Range

Even after equating adjustments are made, no single test score provides a perfectly accurate estimate of your proficiency. Therefore, we provide a score range on the SSAT score scale to emphasize the possibility of score differences if you had taken a different edition of the test instead of the one you took. Your scores on these different versions would likely fall within the scaled score ranges indicated.

Ⓓ SSAT Reference Information

The SSAT is a norm-referenced test. A norm-referenced test interprets an individual test taker's score relative to the distribution of scores for a comparison group, referred to as the *norm group*.

SSAT provides reference information based on two norm groups. The first norm group, indicated as "Grade 8 Total," contains all test takers in the same grade level who have taken one of the Standard administrations in the United States and Canada within the past three years. The second norm group, indicated as "Grade 8 Male," contains test takers of the same grade level and gender who have taken one of the Standard

Continued on Page 60

Secondary School Admission Test Score Report

About You

Student Name
STUDENT, SAMPLE

Grade
8

Gender
Male

Date of Birth
01 Jan 2000

The Test You Took Ⓑ

Registration Number
123456789

SAMPLE STUDENT
1234 Main Street
Anytown, NJ 08888
USA

Test Date
01 Aug 2015

Test Level
Upper

Test Center
SSAT Academy

 Ⓒ Ⓓ

	Your Scaled Scores		SSAT Reference Information					
	Possible Scaled Score Range: 500-800		Grade 8 Total			Grade 8 Male		
	Score	Range	Your Percentile	Average Score	Range	Your Percentile	Average Score	Range
Verbal	752	731-773	92	666	645-687	93	666	645-687
Quantitative	665	644-686	43	675	654-696	41	684	663-705
Reading	701	680-722	80	655	634-676	82	653	632-674
Total	2118		74	1996		75	2003	

What is my Scaled Score, and Why Do I have a Personal Score Range?

Scores are first calculated by awarding one point for each correct answer and subtracting one-quarter of one point for each incorrect answer. These scores are called raw scores. Raw scores can vary from one edition of the test to another due to differences in difficulty among different editions. A statistical procedure called "equating" is used to adjust for these differences. Even after these adjustments, no single test score provides a perfectly accurate estimate of your proficiency. Therefore, we provide a score range on the SSAT score scale to emphasize the possibility of score differences if you had taken a different edition of the test instead of the one you took. Your scores on these different versions would likely fall within the scaled score ranges indicated above.

What Do My SSAT Percentiles Mean?

Your SSAT percentiles have a range of 1 to 99, indicating the percentage of other test takers who scored at or below your scaled score. The first SSAT percentile compares your performance to the performances of all other students in the same grade level who have taken the test in the last three years. The second SSAT percentile compares your performance to the performance of other students of the same grade and gender who have taken the SSAT within the past three years. If you are concerned that your percentiles are lower than you have earned on other tests, please remember that SSAT test takers are members of a small and highly competitive group of students who plan to attend some of the world's best independent schools. You should not be discouraged by what seems to be a lower percentile than you usually attain on standardized tests.

Test Question Breakdown Ⓔ

Verbal
Questions testing your knowledge of words (synonyms) and your ability to relate ideas (analogies).

	Right	Wrong	Not Answered
Synonyms	24	6	0
Analogies	21	9	0

Math
Questions testing your knowledge of number properties and relationships, basic computation, concepts of equivalencies, geometry, measurement, and interpretation of charts/graphs.

	Right	Wrong	Not Answered
Number Concepts & Operations	8	6	8
Algebra, Geometry & Other Math	13	7	8

Reading
Questions regarding the main idea and supporting details of a passage or requiring higher order skills, such as deriving the meaning of words from context, extracting the meaning of a passage, or interpreting an author's logic, attitude and tone.

	Right	Wrong	Not Answered
Main Idea	16	4	0
Higher Order	16	4	0

Questions not answered include both omitted questions and questions not reached. The number of Right, Wrong, and Not Answered questions should NOT be compared across different forms, for the same test taker or between different test takers. The number of Right, Wrong, and Not Answered questions not only depends on a test taker's ability, but also depends on the difficulty of the questions. Hence, score equating is used to adjust the form difficulty differences, and the resulting scaled scores can be compared across forms.

administrations in the United States and Canada within the past three years. The difference between the two norm groups is that the Total norm group contains both male and female test takers, whereas the second norm group is gender specific.

SSAT Percentile Ranks

The SSAT reports percentile ranks. The percentile rank is the percentage of students in the norm group whose scores fall below a particular scaled score. For example, if an 8th grade male student's Verbal scaled score is 698 and the percentile rank is 70 in the total group, it means that 70% of all 8th grade students in the norm group had a Verbal score lower than 698.

Many parents express concern that their child's SSAT percentiles are lower than those they have earned on other tests. Please remember that SSAT test takers are members of a small and highly competitive group of students who plan to attend some of the world's best independent schools. Do not be discouraged by what seems to be a lower score than the student usually attains on standardized testing.

> It is important to remember that SSAT test takers are members of a small and highly competitive group of students who plan to attend some of the world's best private/independent schools. Being in the middle of this group is still impressive!

International and Flex test scores are not included in the comparison group above. While they are not part of the norm group described above, their Scaled Scores are compared to the domestic/Standard/first-time test-taker norm group described above.

SSAT Average Score

SSAT Scaled Score Averages provide additional context information for your SSAT Scaled Score on each of the three scored sections (Verbal, Quantitative/Math, and Reading). These average scores are based on the same two norm groups that are used to provide the SSAT percentiles.

The first SSAT Scaled Score Average is the average performance of all other students in the total norm group. The second SSAT Scaled Score Average is the average performance of all other students in the gender-specific norm group.

These test populations include only those tests taken on one of the eight SSAT Standard test dates in the United States and Canada. For students who have taken the SSAT more than once, only their first set of scores are included.

SSAT Average Score Range

As with SSAT Scaled Scores, no single test score provides a perfectly accurate estimate of proficiency. Therefore, we provide a score range for each of the SSAT Average Scores to emphasize the possibility of score differences if a different edition of the test was taken.

E Test Question Breakdown

This section provides useful and detailed information about the test's content and the student's test-taking strategies. Look carefully at the ratio of wrong answers to unanswered questions. If the student had many wrong answers but omitted few or no questions, meaning that they were guessing quite a bit instead of skipping questions they couldn't answer, that could have an adverse effect on scores.

Parent's Corner: Supporting Your Test Taker

Here are a few simple things you can do to help your student perform as well as possible on the Upper Level SSAT without creating too much anxiety.

Practice! Practice! Practice! Help your student structure practice time to take the Upper Level SSAT Practice Tests in the next chapter. Act as the proctor—administer the timed practice tests while approximating the standard testing conditions as closely as possible (no notes, no talking, no computer, no calculator).

Review and encourage! Review any incorrect answers that your student chose. Which sections or types of questions proved most difficult for your student to answer? Focus, encourage, and help your student sharpen those skills. Examine your student's guessing strategy. Try to figure out the cause of the errors so that your student can develop a strategy for avoiding similar mistakes on the actual test.

Some common pitfalls:
- Accidentally marking the wrong circle on the answer sheet even when the student knows the correct answer
- Making simple arithmetic mistakes

Double-checking answers and not rushing can help with this.

Extra help! If taking the practice tests reveals that your student lacks a particular skill that is necessary for success, seeking extra help for your student may be useful.

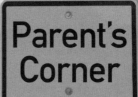

Perspective is everything! Keep the importance of the SSAT in perspective and help your student do the same. The SSAT is an important and valuable part of the application package and students should prepare for it. But remember that the SSAT is just *one* part of the entire package. Schools will weigh your student's test scores along with other information.

Retaking the test? Should your student want to retake the Upper Level SSAT, many options are available. Scores tend to vary if your student retakes the test. In general, the lower the initial scores, the more likely the scores will increase the second time.

Rest up and eat well! Make sure your student gets enough sleep on the days leading up to the test and that he or she eats a healthy breakfast on the day it is administered.

Be prepared for the unexpected! If your student panics, freezes, or gets sick during the administration of the SSAT, she or he has the option to leave the test. It's important for you to know that if your child does leave the test, the results will be cancelled. It's your responsibility, however, to alert SSATB immediately so that the scores are voided and not sent to schools. Please note that your fee for the cancelled test will not be refunded, but for a service charge, you may reschedule for a new test date.

THIS PAGE INTENTIONALLY LEFT BLANK.

Upper Level Practice Tests

THIS PAGE INTENTIONALLY LEFT BLANK.

Trying Out the Upper Level SSAT

Now it's time to find out what it's actually like to take the Upper Level SSAT. Ask a parent or other adult to help you set up a simulation—a recreation of the experience that is as close as possible to actually taking the Upper Level SSAT. Think of it as a dress rehearsal for the real thing. Simulating the SSAT experience can help you walk into the testing center with more confidence and clarity about what to expect.

Remove (or photocopy) the answer sheet and use it to complete each practice test.

You can choose to do your simulation section by section or by taking an entire test from start to finish.

Here are the rules you'll need to follow to make your SSAT simulation as realistic as possible:

- Ask your "test proctor" to keep time and tell you when to begin and end each section.

- No talking or music is allowed during the SSAT, so make sure the room in which you are taking the test is quiet, and turn off anything that makes noise, such as your phone, iPod, or TV.

- You will not be allowed to use any research material while taking the Upper Level SSAT, so put away your smartphone, laptop, books, dictionary, calculator, ruler, and notes.

- Work only on one section during the time allotted. Do not go back to another section to finish unanswered questions.

- Use sharpened #2 pencils with erasers.

- Fill in the answer sheet (located before each test in the book) just as you would during a regular test.

Simulating the Test: Section by Section

If your goal is to sharpen your test-taking techniques in a specific area, use the individual sections for the simulation. Review the exercises in Chapter 2 before beginning, and be sure to follow the instructions for each section carefully. Schedule the allotted time for each section, and ask the person supervising your simulation to time you, or set a timer for yourself.

As you will when you actually take the Upper Level SSAT, mark your answer choices on the answer sheet.

Simulating the Test: Start to Finish

If your goal is to practice taking the entire Upper Level SSAT (minus the experimental section), here's how to schedule your time blocks, including breaks:

Test Overview		
Section	**Number of Questions**	**Time Allotted To Administer Each Section**
Writing Sample	1	25 minutes
Break		5 minutes
Section 1 (Quantitative)	25	30 minutes
Section 2 (Reading)	40	40 minutes
Break		10 minutes
Section 3 (Verbal)	60	30 minutes
Section 4 (Quantitative)	25	30 minutes
Totals	151	**2 hours, 50 minutes**

When you add this all up, you'll see that the total testing time is 2 hours and 35 minutes. When you add in the two breaks, the total time is 2 hours and 50 minutes (these practice tests do not include an experimental section). Be sure to use your breaks for stretching, getting a drink of water, and focusing your eyes on something other than a test paper. This will help clear your mind and get you ready for the next section.

A note about special timing: Students who have disabilities may apply for and be granted testing accommodations. Some students are granted "time and a half," and they are given 1.5 times the minutes available for each test section—including the writing sample. However, students who are granted 1.5x time do not take the experimental section.

Practice Test I: Upper Level Answer Sheet

Be sure each mark completely fills the answer space.

Start with number 1 for each new section of the test. You may find more answer spaces than you need.
If so, please leave them blank.

Section 1

1 Ⓐ Ⓑ Ⓒ Ⓓ Ⓔ	6 Ⓐ Ⓑ Ⓒ Ⓓ Ⓔ	11 Ⓐ Ⓑ Ⓒ Ⓓ Ⓔ	16 Ⓐ Ⓑ Ⓒ Ⓓ Ⓔ	21 Ⓐ Ⓑ Ⓒ Ⓓ Ⓔ
2 Ⓐ Ⓑ Ⓒ Ⓓ Ⓔ	7 Ⓐ Ⓑ Ⓒ Ⓓ Ⓔ	12 Ⓐ Ⓑ Ⓒ Ⓓ Ⓔ	17 Ⓐ Ⓑ Ⓒ Ⓓ Ⓔ	22 Ⓐ Ⓑ Ⓒ Ⓓ Ⓔ
3 Ⓐ Ⓑ Ⓒ Ⓓ Ⓔ	8 Ⓐ Ⓑ Ⓒ Ⓓ Ⓔ	13 Ⓐ Ⓑ Ⓒ Ⓓ Ⓔ	18 Ⓐ Ⓑ Ⓒ Ⓓ Ⓔ	23 Ⓐ Ⓑ Ⓒ Ⓓ Ⓔ
4 Ⓐ Ⓑ Ⓒ Ⓓ Ⓔ	9 Ⓐ Ⓑ Ⓒ Ⓓ Ⓔ	14 Ⓐ Ⓑ Ⓒ Ⓓ Ⓔ	19 Ⓐ Ⓑ Ⓒ Ⓓ Ⓔ	24 Ⓐ Ⓑ Ⓒ Ⓓ Ⓔ
5 Ⓐ Ⓑ Ⓒ Ⓓ Ⓔ	10 Ⓐ Ⓑ Ⓒ Ⓓ Ⓔ	15 Ⓐ Ⓑ Ⓒ Ⓓ Ⓔ	20 Ⓐ Ⓑ Ⓒ Ⓓ Ⓔ	25 Ⓐ Ⓑ Ⓒ Ⓓ Ⓔ

Section 2

1 Ⓐ Ⓑ Ⓒ Ⓓ Ⓔ	9 Ⓐ Ⓑ Ⓒ Ⓓ Ⓔ	17 Ⓐ Ⓑ Ⓒ Ⓓ Ⓔ	25 Ⓐ Ⓑ Ⓒ Ⓓ Ⓔ	33 Ⓐ Ⓑ Ⓒ Ⓓ Ⓔ
2 Ⓐ Ⓑ Ⓒ Ⓓ Ⓔ	10 Ⓐ Ⓑ Ⓒ Ⓓ Ⓔ	18 Ⓐ Ⓑ Ⓒ Ⓓ Ⓔ	26 Ⓐ Ⓑ Ⓒ Ⓓ Ⓔ	34 Ⓐ Ⓑ Ⓒ Ⓓ Ⓔ
3 Ⓐ Ⓑ Ⓒ Ⓓ Ⓔ	11 Ⓐ Ⓑ Ⓒ Ⓓ Ⓔ	19 Ⓐ Ⓑ Ⓒ Ⓓ Ⓔ	27 Ⓐ Ⓑ Ⓒ Ⓓ Ⓔ	35 Ⓐ Ⓑ Ⓒ Ⓓ Ⓔ
4 Ⓐ Ⓑ Ⓒ Ⓓ Ⓔ	12 Ⓐ Ⓑ Ⓒ Ⓓ Ⓔ	20 Ⓐ Ⓑ Ⓒ Ⓓ Ⓔ	28 Ⓐ Ⓑ Ⓒ Ⓓ Ⓔ	36 Ⓐ Ⓑ Ⓒ Ⓓ Ⓔ
5 Ⓐ Ⓑ Ⓒ Ⓓ Ⓔ	13 Ⓐ Ⓑ Ⓒ Ⓓ Ⓔ	21 Ⓐ Ⓑ Ⓒ Ⓓ Ⓔ	29 Ⓐ Ⓑ Ⓒ Ⓓ Ⓔ	37 Ⓐ Ⓑ Ⓒ Ⓓ Ⓔ
6 Ⓐ Ⓑ Ⓒ Ⓓ Ⓔ	14 Ⓐ Ⓑ Ⓒ Ⓓ Ⓔ	22 Ⓐ Ⓑ Ⓒ Ⓓ Ⓔ	30 Ⓐ Ⓑ Ⓒ Ⓓ Ⓔ	38 Ⓐ Ⓑ Ⓒ Ⓓ Ⓔ
7 Ⓐ Ⓑ Ⓒ Ⓓ Ⓔ	15 Ⓐ Ⓑ Ⓒ Ⓓ Ⓔ	23 Ⓐ Ⓑ Ⓒ Ⓓ Ⓔ	31 Ⓐ Ⓑ Ⓒ Ⓓ Ⓔ	39 Ⓐ Ⓑ Ⓒ Ⓓ Ⓔ
8 Ⓐ Ⓑ Ⓒ Ⓓ Ⓔ	16 Ⓐ Ⓑ Ⓒ Ⓓ Ⓔ	24 Ⓐ Ⓑ Ⓒ Ⓓ Ⓔ	32 Ⓐ Ⓑ Ⓒ Ⓓ Ⓔ	40 Ⓐ Ⓑ Ⓒ Ⓓ Ⓔ

Section 3

1 Ⓐ Ⓑ Ⓒ Ⓓ Ⓔ	13 Ⓐ Ⓑ Ⓒ Ⓓ Ⓔ	25 Ⓐ Ⓑ Ⓒ Ⓓ Ⓔ	37 Ⓐ Ⓑ Ⓒ Ⓓ Ⓔ	49 Ⓐ Ⓑ Ⓒ Ⓓ Ⓔ
2 Ⓐ Ⓑ Ⓒ Ⓓ Ⓔ	14 Ⓐ Ⓑ Ⓒ Ⓓ Ⓔ	26 Ⓐ Ⓑ Ⓒ Ⓓ Ⓔ	38 Ⓐ Ⓑ Ⓒ Ⓓ Ⓔ	50 Ⓐ Ⓑ Ⓒ Ⓓ Ⓔ
3 Ⓐ Ⓑ Ⓒ Ⓓ Ⓔ	15 Ⓐ Ⓑ Ⓒ Ⓓ Ⓔ	27 Ⓐ Ⓑ Ⓒ Ⓓ Ⓔ	39 Ⓐ Ⓑ Ⓒ Ⓓ Ⓔ	51 Ⓐ Ⓑ Ⓒ Ⓓ Ⓔ
4 Ⓐ Ⓑ Ⓒ Ⓓ Ⓔ	16 Ⓐ Ⓑ Ⓒ Ⓓ Ⓔ	28 Ⓐ Ⓑ Ⓒ Ⓓ Ⓔ	40 Ⓐ Ⓑ Ⓒ Ⓓ Ⓔ	52 Ⓐ Ⓑ Ⓒ Ⓓ Ⓔ
5 Ⓐ Ⓑ Ⓒ Ⓓ Ⓔ	17 Ⓐ Ⓑ Ⓒ Ⓓ Ⓔ	29 Ⓐ Ⓑ Ⓒ Ⓓ Ⓔ	41 Ⓐ Ⓑ Ⓒ Ⓓ Ⓔ	53 Ⓐ Ⓑ Ⓒ Ⓓ Ⓔ
6 Ⓐ Ⓑ Ⓒ Ⓓ Ⓔ	18 Ⓐ Ⓑ Ⓒ Ⓓ Ⓔ	30 Ⓐ Ⓑ Ⓒ Ⓓ Ⓔ	42 Ⓐ Ⓑ Ⓒ Ⓓ Ⓔ	54 Ⓐ Ⓑ Ⓒ Ⓓ Ⓔ
7 Ⓐ Ⓑ Ⓒ Ⓓ Ⓔ	19 Ⓐ Ⓑ Ⓒ Ⓓ Ⓔ	31 Ⓐ Ⓑ Ⓒ Ⓓ Ⓔ	43 Ⓐ Ⓑ Ⓒ Ⓓ Ⓔ	55 Ⓐ Ⓑ Ⓒ Ⓓ Ⓔ
8 Ⓐ Ⓑ Ⓒ Ⓓ Ⓔ	20 Ⓐ Ⓑ Ⓒ Ⓓ Ⓔ	32 Ⓐ Ⓑ Ⓒ Ⓓ Ⓔ	44 Ⓐ Ⓑ Ⓒ Ⓓ Ⓔ	56 Ⓐ Ⓑ Ⓒ Ⓓ Ⓔ
9 Ⓐ Ⓑ Ⓒ Ⓓ Ⓔ	21 Ⓐ Ⓑ Ⓒ Ⓓ Ⓔ	33 Ⓐ Ⓑ Ⓒ Ⓓ Ⓔ	45 Ⓐ Ⓑ Ⓒ Ⓓ Ⓔ	57 Ⓐ Ⓑ Ⓒ Ⓓ Ⓔ
10 Ⓐ Ⓑ Ⓒ Ⓓ Ⓔ	22 Ⓐ Ⓑ Ⓒ Ⓓ Ⓔ	34 Ⓐ Ⓑ Ⓒ Ⓓ Ⓔ	46 Ⓐ Ⓑ Ⓒ Ⓓ Ⓔ	58 Ⓐ Ⓑ Ⓒ Ⓓ Ⓔ
11 Ⓐ Ⓑ Ⓒ Ⓓ Ⓔ	23 Ⓐ Ⓑ Ⓒ Ⓓ Ⓔ	35 Ⓐ Ⓑ Ⓒ Ⓓ Ⓔ	47 Ⓐ Ⓑ Ⓒ Ⓓ Ⓔ	59 Ⓐ Ⓑ Ⓒ Ⓓ Ⓔ
12 Ⓐ Ⓑ Ⓒ Ⓓ Ⓔ	24 Ⓐ Ⓑ Ⓒ Ⓓ Ⓔ	36 Ⓐ Ⓑ Ⓒ Ⓓ Ⓔ	48 Ⓐ Ⓑ Ⓒ Ⓓ Ⓔ	60 Ⓐ Ⓑ Ⓒ Ⓓ Ⓔ

Section 4

1 Ⓐ Ⓑ Ⓒ Ⓓ Ⓔ	6 Ⓐ Ⓑ Ⓒ Ⓓ Ⓔ	11 Ⓐ Ⓑ Ⓒ Ⓓ Ⓔ	16 Ⓐ Ⓑ Ⓒ Ⓓ Ⓔ	21 Ⓐ Ⓑ Ⓒ Ⓓ Ⓔ
2 Ⓐ Ⓑ Ⓒ Ⓓ Ⓔ	7 Ⓐ Ⓑ Ⓒ Ⓓ Ⓔ	12 Ⓐ Ⓑ Ⓒ Ⓓ Ⓔ	17 Ⓐ Ⓑ Ⓒ Ⓓ Ⓔ	22 Ⓐ Ⓑ Ⓒ Ⓓ Ⓔ
3 Ⓐ Ⓑ Ⓒ Ⓓ Ⓔ	8 Ⓐ Ⓑ Ⓒ Ⓓ Ⓔ	13 Ⓐ Ⓑ Ⓒ Ⓓ Ⓔ	18 Ⓐ Ⓑ Ⓒ Ⓓ Ⓔ	23 Ⓐ Ⓑ Ⓒ Ⓓ Ⓔ
4 Ⓐ Ⓑ Ⓒ Ⓓ Ⓔ	9 Ⓐ Ⓑ Ⓒ Ⓓ Ⓔ	14 Ⓐ Ⓑ Ⓒ Ⓓ Ⓔ	19 Ⓐ Ⓑ Ⓒ Ⓓ Ⓔ	24 Ⓐ Ⓑ Ⓒ Ⓓ Ⓔ
5 Ⓐ Ⓑ Ⓒ Ⓓ Ⓔ	10 Ⓐ Ⓑ Ⓒ Ⓓ Ⓔ	15 Ⓐ Ⓑ Ⓒ Ⓓ Ⓔ	20 Ⓐ Ⓑ Ⓒ Ⓓ Ⓔ	25 Ⓐ Ⓑ Ⓒ Ⓓ Ⓔ

Section 5

Experimental Section – See page 11 for details.

THIS PAGE INTENTIONALLY LEFT BLANK.

Writing Sample

Schools would like to get to know you better through an essay or story you write using one of the two topics below. Please select the topic you find most interesting and fill in the circle next to the topic you choose.

Ⓐ Which three literary figures would you invite to dinner and why?

Ⓑ The silence was overwhelming.

Use this page and the next page to complete your writing sample.

Continue on next page.

SECTION 1
25 Questions

Following each problem in this section, there are five suggested answers. Work each problem in your head or in the blank space provided at the right of the page. Then look at the five suggested answers and decide which one is best.

<u>Note:</u> Figures that accompany problems in this section are drawn as accurately as possible EXCEPT when it is stated in a specific problem that its figure is not drawn to scale.

Sample Problem:

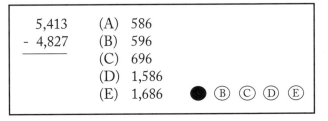

5,413	(A) 586
- 4,827	(B) 596
	(C) 696
	(D) 1,586
	(E) 1,686

USE THIS SPACE FOR FIGURING.

1. Jimmy plans to buy a beach ball for every one of his 13 staff members for their end-of-year party. There are three beach balls in each package. How many packages must he buy?

   (A) 2
   (B) 4
   (C) 5
   (D) 6
   (E) 10

---

2. Estimate the total amount of rain that fell during 8 hours of Hurricane Irene, according to the table.

   (A) 7 cm
   (B) 13 cm
   (C) 14 cm
   (D) 20 cm
   (E) 24 cm

Hurricane Irene

Hour	cm of rain
1	0.1
2	0.5
3	2.3
4	6.9
5	7.0
6	3.5
7	2.5
8	0.3

GO ON TO THE NEXT PAGE.

USE THIS SPACE FOR FIGURING.

3. Which figure can be drawn without lifting the pencil or retracing?

   (A)

   (B)

   (C)

   (D)

   (E)

4. Jennifer earns a base hourly rate of $8 per hour at her job. However, if she works more than 10 hours in a week, she earns $9 per hour for each hour she works after the first 10 hours. How much money does Jennifer earn if she works 16 hours in one week?

   (A) $128
   (B) $134
   (C) $135
   (D) $138
   (E) $144

5. Fred has a sticks more than Annie. Annie has 7 sticks. How many sticks does Fred have?

   (A) $a - 7$
   (B) $7 + a$
   (C) $\frac{a}{7}$
   (D) $7 - a$
   (E) $\frac{7}{a}$

6. A small cube has a side length of 2 inches. How many small cubes are needed to make a larger cube whose base has a perimeter of 32 inches?

   (A) 8
   (B) 16
   (C) 32
   (D) 64
   (E) 192

GO ON TO THE NEXT PAGE.

USE THIS SPACE FOR FIGURING.

7. Which of the following could be the value of A if $\frac{1}{5} + A > 1$?

   (A) $\frac{1}{5}$

   (B) $\frac{2}{5}$

   (C) $\frac{2}{3}$

   (D) $\frac{1}{2}$

   (E) $\frac{9}{10}$

Questions 8-9 are based on the table in the figure.

8. The fractional part of the number of biologists employed in education in year X was approximately

   (A) $\frac{1}{4}$

   (B) $\frac{7}{20}$

   (C) $\frac{1}{2}$

   (D) $\frac{3}{5}$

   (E) $\frac{7}{10}$

9. If the number of engineers in the United States in year X was 30,000, approximately what was the difference in the number of engineers in government and the number in education?

   (A) 5,000

   (B) 6,000

   (C) 7,000

   (D) 15,000

   (E) 22,500

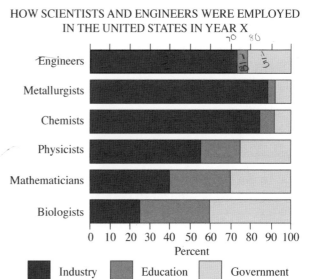

HOW SCIENTISTS AND ENGINEERS WERE EMPLOYED IN THE UNITED STATES IN YEAR X

GO ON TO THE NEXT PAGE.

USE THIS SPACE FOR FIGURING.

10. Heather is collecting dimes. She saves one dime on the first day, two dimes on the second day, and three dimes on the third day. If this pattern continues, how much money will Heather have saved at the end of 30 days?

(A) $45.50

(B) $46.00

(C) $46.10

(D) $46.50

(E) $47.50

11. When $A + B = 13$ and $2D + B = 13$, what is the value of D?

(A) 13

(B) 5

(C) –5

(D) –7

(E) It cannot be determined from the information given.

12. In the figure, segment PQ is 45 centimeters long. How long is segment RQ?

(A) 15 cm

(B) 18 cm

(C) 24 cm

(D) 27 cm

(E) 30 cm

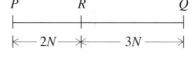

$$\frac{87,412}{3,024} =$$

13. The result of the above calculation is closest to which of the following?

(A) 30

(B) 2,900

(C) 30,000

(D) 85,000

(E) 90,000

GO ON TO THE NEXT PAGE.

USE THIS SPACE FOR FIGURING.

14. The mass required to trigger a mouse trap is 157g. What is the largest mass of cheese a 4 oz. mouse could carry and not set off the trap? (1 oz. = 28g)

(A) 28g

(B) 44g

(C) 45g

(D) 56g

(E) 112g

---

15. $\sqrt[4]{a^9}$ =

(A) $36a$

(B) a^3

(C) a^5

(D) a^{36}

(E) $(a^2)\sqrt[4]{a}$

---

16. If 30% of a number is 150, then 70% of that same number is

(A) 70

(B) 100

(C) 190

(D) 350

(E) 2100

---

17. If the points $(4, 2)$ and $(-1, k)$ are on a line that is perpendicular to the line $y = 2x + 1$, what is the value of k?

(A) $-\frac{1}{2}$

(B) $-\frac{7}{2}$

(C) $\frac{9}{2}$

(D) $\frac{7}{2}$

(E) 12

GO ON TO THE NEXT PAGE.

USE THIS SPACE FOR FIGURING.

18. The figure shows an L-shaped triple. Which game board can be completely covered by placing L-shaped triples on the board without overlapping?

(A)

(B)

(C)

(D)

(E)

19. A circle, a square, and an equilateral triangle all have the same perimeter. Which of the following lists the shapes in increasing order of area?

(A) circle, square, triangle
(B) circle, triangle, square
(C) triangle, circle, square
(D) square, triangle, circle
(E) triangle, square, circle

20. A parking lot owner sold 20% of the area of his lot to his neighbor. Later that year he sold 20% of the remainder of his lot to another neighbor. What percent of his original parking area does he now have?

(A) 16%
(B) 40%
(C) 60%
(D) 64%
(E) 80%

GO ON TO THE NEXT PAGE.

USE THIS SPACE FOR FIGURING.

21. If the dots in the figure shown are connected by starting at 1 and then going to 2, it will be necessary to retrace a line or lift the pencil to draw which figure?

(A)

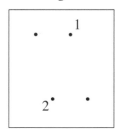

(B)

(C)

(D)

(E)

22. If 60 percent of t is 8, what is 30 percent of $2t$?

(A) 2
(B) 4
(C) 8
(D) 16
(E) 24

23. Let x be an integer such that $1 < x < 12$. What is the probability that x is divisible by 3 but NOT divisible by 2?

(A) $\frac{1}{6}$
(B) $\frac{1}{5}$
(C) $\frac{3}{10}$
(D) $\frac{1}{3}$
(E) $\frac{7}{10}$

GO ON TO THE NEXT PAGE.

USE THIS SPACE FOR FIGURING.

24. If the average of five consecutive whole numbers is 18, what is the smallest number?

    (A) 8
    (B) 12
    (C) 16
    (D) 17
    (E) 18

25. A movie theater has an average of 400 customers per day. To increase business, the owner plans to reduce the regular price from $8.00 to $6.00 before 6 p.m. each day. If 100 people pay $8.00, how many people must pay $6.00 if daily sales are to remain the same as before the $6.00 price reduction plan?

    (A) 360
    (B) 400
    (C) 420
    (D) 480
    (E) 500

STOP
**IF YOU FINISH BEFORE TIME IS CALLED,
YOU MAY CHECK YOUR WORK ON THIS SECTION ONLY.
DO NOT TURN TO ANY OTHER SECTION IN THE TEST.**

SECTION 2
40 Questions

Read each passage carefully and then answer the questions about it. For each question, decide on the basis of the passage which one of the choices best answers the question.

> Mr. Duffy lived in Chapelizod because he wished to live as far as possible from the city of which he was a citizen and because he found all other suburbs of Dublin mean, modern, and pretentious. He had been for many years cashier of a private bank in Baggot Street. Every morning he came in from Chapelizod by streetcar. At midday
> *Line 5* he went to Dan Burke's and took his lunch—a bottle of lager beer and a small trayful of arrowroot biscuits. At four o'clock he was set free. He dined in an eating house on George's Street where he felt himself safe from the society of Dublin's gilded youth and where there was a certain plain honesty in the bill of fare. His evenings were spent either before his landlady's piano or roaming about the outskirts of the city. His liking
> *10* for Mozart's music brought him sometimes to an opera or a concert. These were the only dissipations of his life.

1. The author's primary purpose in the passage is to
   (A) resolve a plot
   (B) create suspense
   (C) describe city life
   (D) describe a scene
   (E) describe a character

2. Why did Mr. Duffy prefer Chapelizod to the other suburbs of Dublin?
   (A) It was closer to Dan Burke's.
   (B) It offered modern conveniences.
   (C) It was where his business was located.
   (D) It was a place where he was not known.
   (E) It was unpretentious and remote from Dublin.

3. Mr. Duffy's chief diversion apparently was
   (A) work
   (B) music
   (C) travel
   (D) the theater
   (E) good company

4. As he is described in the passage, Mr. Duffy appears to be
   (A) cruel
   (B) degenerate
   (C) a creature of habit
   (D) a remorseful person
   (E) a man of many interests

GO ON TO THE NEXT PAGE.

Being small, solitary, herbivorous, and cuddly has not been much help to the koala. Long before it could blame its troubles on an airline advertising campaign, the two-foot tall Australian marsupial was hunted almost to extinction for its furry pelt. Only since the koala was declared a protected species in the late 1920's has it made something of a comeback. So

Line 5   perhaps the koala could be forgiven for thinking that life might be more bearable if it was closer to the size of a real bear.

In fact, it once was. Rooting around a southern Australian cave in 1985, spelunker Graham Pilkington uncovered a fossilized jaw fragment of a creature later identified as a giant koala, which probably inhabited the continent more than 1 million years ago. The

10   jawbone and front molars are about twice the size of those of a present-day koala. This suggests that the creature was more than three feet tall and weighed between 45 and 65 pounds. Not exactly a grizzly bear, but about two to three times as heavy as modern koalas.

Still, as the curator of fossils at the South Australian Museum explains, this larger size may have been a mixed blessing. Although the giant koala was perhaps better equipped to

15   ward off foes, it probably subsisted on the same diet of eucalyptus leaves its descendants favor. Not all eucalyptus branches could have supported that much weight, so dining out could have been an adventure for a giant koala. Worse still, late in the Pleistocene period, a series of droughts ravaged southeastern Australia, wiping out many species including the giant koala. Hardier and requiring less sustenance, only smaller members of the koala family survived.

5. The author's use of which of the following words is an example of a pun?

   (A) solitary (line 1)
   (B) hunted (line 3)
   (C) pelt (line 3)
   (D) bearable (line 5)
   (E) favor (line 15)

6. In which of the following does the author speak of the koala as if it were human?

   (A) "Being small, solitary, herbivorous, and cuddly has not been much help to the koala."
   (B) "The koala could be forgiven for thinking that life might be more bearable if it were closer to the size of a real bear."
   (C) "The jawbone and front molars are about twice the size of those of a present-day koala."
   (D) "This larger size may have been a mixed blessing."
   (E) "It probably subsisted on the same diet of eucalyptus leaves its descendants favor."

7. "Rooting around" (line 7) could be replaced by which of the following without changing the author's meaning?

   (A) Camping near
   (B) Hurrying through
   (C) Striding toward
   (D) Falling into
   (E) Poking about

8. In line 15, "its" refers to the

   (A) grizzly bear
   (B) South Australian Museum
   (C) giant koala
   (D) eucalyptus leaf
   (E) diet

9. The passage contains information to answer which of the following questions?

   (A) How many front molars did the giant koala have?
   (B) How long ago did the giant koalas probably live in Australia?
   (C) How did the giant koala defend itself against its enemies?
   (D) What were the pelts of koalas used for?
   (E) What are the troubles that the present-day koala blames on an airline advertising campaign?

10. According to the passage, which of the following is true of the giant koalas?

   (A) They were not able to climb eucalyptus trees.
   (B) They were less than two feet tall.
   (C) They were frequently attacked by other animals.
   (D) They became extinct during the Pleistocene period.
   (E) They became a protected species in the 1920's.

GO ON TO THE NEXT PAGE.

Many people suppose the situation in an operating room to be like this: the atmosphere is tense; scarcely a word is spoken. The surgeon dominates the entire room with a powerful personality and expresses with authority quiet, terse commands, "Scalpel!"– "Scissors!"–"Sponge!"–"Hemostat!" The rest of the team say nothing, but
Line 5   carry out the orders like automatons.
An operating room actually is not at all like this. What is happening is that the changing needs of the patient, as they develop in the course of the operation, determine what everybody does. When a surgical team has worked long enough together to develop true teamwork, each member has such a grasp of the total situation and his or
10   her role in it that the needs of the patient give unequivocal orders.
A small artery is cut and begins to bleed. In a chain-of-command organization, the surgeon would note this and say to the attendant, "Stop that bleeder." The assistant in turn would say to the surgical nurse, "Give me a hemostat," and thus, coordinated effort would be achieved. What actually happens is that the bleeder gives a simultaneous
15   command to all three members of the team, all of whom have been watching the progress of the operation with equal attention. It says to the surgeon, "Get your hand out of the way until this is controlled." It says to the instrument nurse, "Get a hemostat ready," and it says to the assistant, "Clamp that off." This is the highest and most efficient type of cooperation known. It is possible only where every member of the team
20   knows enough about the total job and that of each other member to see the relationship of what he or she does to everything else that goes on.

11. In an operating room, the course of an operation depends mostly on the

(A) patient
(B) surgeon
(C) surgical nurse
(D) instrument nurse
(E) surgeon's assistant

12. A hemostat is used to

(A) soak up blood
(B) stitch a wound
(C) cut blood vessels
(D) clamp off blood vessels
(E) hold the surgeon's hand steady

13. Which of the following qualities is most desirable for the head of a surgical team?

(A) a powerful personality
(B) an authoritative voice
(C) the ability to give forceful orders
(D) a thorough knowledge of surgery
(E) the ability to get along with patients

14. The actual clamping off of arteries during an operation is apparently the job of the

(A) surgeon
(B) surgical team
(C) surgical nurse
(D) instrument nurse
(E) surgeon's assistant

15. This passage was probably written to

(A) describe a particular operation
(B) correct a false idea about operating room procedures
(C) enumerate the conditions necessary for good teamwork
(D) instruct surgeons as to the best way to control bleeding in a patient
(E) instruct new members of a surgical team on operating room procedures

GO ON TO THE NEXT PAGE.

The following speech was delivered by Susan B. Anthony at her trial in 1873.

Friends and fellow-citizens: I stand before you tonight under indictment for the alleged crime of having voted at the last Presidential election [1872], without having a lawful right to vote. It shall be my work this evening to prove to you that in thus voting, I not only committed no crime, but, instead, simply exercised my citizen's rights, guaranteed
Line 5 to me and all United States citizens by the National Constitution.

It was we, the people; not we, the White male citizens; nor yet we, the male citizens; but we, the whole people, who formed the Union. And we formed it, not to give the blessings of liberty, but to secure them; not to the half of ourselves but to the whole people—women as well as men. And it is a downright mockery to talk to women of their
10 enjoyment of the blessings of liberty, while they are denied the use of the only means of securing them …—the ballot….

The only question left to be settled now is: Are women persons? And I hardly believe any of our opponents will have the hardihood to say they are not. Being persons, then, women are citizens; and no State has a right to make any law, or to enforce any old law, that
15 shall abridge their privileges or immunities.

16. In line 1, Anthony's use of "fellow-citizens" is ironic for which of the following reasons?

    (A) She was not fully a citizen because she had no right to vote.
    (B) The audience included people not of her sex, race, or religion.
    (C) Most of the citizens in the audience were females.
    (D) Those in the audience who were her friends were not necessarily citizens.
    (E) At that time women were not allowed to make speeches on public issues.

17. What does Anthony mean by "I stand before you tonight under indictment" (line 1)?

    (A) She had been framed by her opponents.
    (B) She was already in jail.
    (C) She had been falsely accused of voting in the last election.
    (D) She was on trial and might be sent to prison.
    (E) She had been allowed to speak by special permission.

18. How does Anthony's speech reflect the idea in a speech by Abraham Lincoln in which he defended "government of the people, by the people, for the people"?

    (A) It points out that all citizens should be able to elect their government.
    (B) It shows that educated women can solve the problems of government.

    (C) It shows that women can have only a theoretical interest in affairs of state.
    (D) It shows that by voting Anthony was overreaching her rights as a citizen.
    (E) It demonstrates that laws in violation of the Constitution are null and void.

19. Why does Anthony say that women's right to vote is guaranteed by the Constitution?

    (A) The Constitution explicitly gave women the right to vote.
    (B) One of the blessings of liberty is being allowed to vote.
    (C) The Constitution gave states the power to authorize women to vote.
    (D) Only children and criminals were denied the right to vote.
    (E) The Constitution begins, "We, the people," which includes women.

20. The purpose of Anthony's speech was to

    (A) influence the women on the jury in her favor
    (B) prove that the right to vote would produce racial equality
    (C) demonstrate that she and other women had the right to vote
    (D) convince people of the need for economic justice: equal pay for equal work
    (E) convince the jury that voting was only a tool to be used by women to gain other rights

GO ON TO THE NEXT PAGE.

Approximately 28 percent of all energy used in the United States is devoted to transportation and of that fraction, 40 percent is supplied in the form of gasoline to fuel the nation's nearly 255 million registered passenger vehicles. Americans use more energy to fuel their cars than they do for any other single purpose. The fuel used by

Line 5 American automobiles and personal trucks would just about fill all the energy needs of Japan, a nation of over 127 million and the world's largest consumer of energy after the United States and China. In an urgent effort to reduce consumption of an increasingly costly fuel whose chief reserves lie overseas, the government has rightly identified the American automobile and current habits of its utilization as prime targets for change.

21. This passage was probably taken from

(A) a historical novel
(B) a speech in a play
(C) an editorial analysis
(D) a gasoline commercial
(E) a government contract

22. According to the passage, Japan's gasoline consumption is

(A) equal to that of China
(B) 127 million gallons a year
(C) equal to that of the United States
(D) less than that of the United States
(E) larger than that of any other country

23. This passage is mostly about

(A) energy needs of Japan
(B) alternative energy sources
(C) car sales in the United States
(D) the extent of oil reserves overseas
(E) gasoline consumption in the United States

24. The passage provides information to answer which of the following questions?

(A) How can current driving habits in the United States be changed?
(B) How many Chinese have automobiles or personal trucks?
(C) What proportion of United States energy is used for transportation?
(D) How are various countries meeting their energy needs?
(E) When will the world's oil supply run out?

GO ON TO THE NEXT PAGE.

The plan which I adopted, and the one by which I was most successful, was that of making friends of all the little white boys whom I met in the street. As many of these as I could, I converted into teachers. With their kindly aid, obtained at different times and in different places, I finally succeeded in learning to read. When I was sent on errands, I
Line 5 always took my book with me, and by going one part of my errand quickly, I found time to get a lesson before my return. I used also to carry bread with me, enough of which was always in the house, and to which I was always welcome; for I was much better off in this regard than many of the poor white children in our neighborhood. This bread I used to bestow upon the hungry little urchins, who, in return, would give me that more
10 valuable bread of knowledge. I am strongly tempted to give the names of two or three of those little boys, as a testimonial of the gratitude and affection I bear them; but prudence forbids;—not that it would injure me, but it might embarrass them; for it is almost an unpardonable offence to teach slaves to read in this Christian country. It is enough to say of the dear little fellows, that they lived on Philpot Street, very near Durgin and Bailey's
15 ship-yard. I used to talk this matter of slavery over with them. I would sometimes say to them, I wished I could be as free as they would be when they got to be men. "You will be free as soon as you are twenty-one,—but I am a slave for life!—Have not I as good a right to be free as you have?" These words used to trouble them; they would express for me the liveliest sympathy, and console me with the hope that something would occur by which I might be free.

25. In lines 9-10 the phrase "that more valuable bread of knowledge" is an example of

(A) hyperbole
(B) metaphor
(C) allegory
(D) synecdoche
(E) personification

26. In line 11, "prudence" most likely means

(A) fear
(B) caution
(C) indifference
(D) pragmatism
(E) carelessness

27. In referring to "this Christian country" (line 13), the author's tone is

(A) ironic
(B) pleasant
(C) forgiving
(D) charitable
(E) superficial

28. The passage implies that the author considers literacy to be the equivalent of

(A) food
(B) liberty
(C) religion
(D) teaching
(E) friendship

29. Which of the following most accurately states the main idea of the passage?

(A) It was socially acceptable for white and black children to interact.
(B) The author discovered an effective alternative to formalized education.
(C) The author was able to trick the children, demonstrating his superior intellect.
(D) The author, though a slave, encountered exceptional children; this was not the norm.
(E) The strong Christian values in America compensated for the difficulties the author encountered because of slavery.

GO ON TO THE NEXT PAGE.

I am not sure that I can draw an exact line between wit and humor, but I am positive that humor is the more comfortable and livable quality. Humorous persons, if their gift is genuine, are always agreeable companions and they sit through the evening best. They have pleasant mouths turned up at the corners. To those corners the great Master of marionettes

Line 5   has fixed the strings and holds them with nimble fingers that twitch them at the slightest jest. But the mouth of a merely witty person is hard and sour until the moment of its discharge. Nor is the flash from a witty person always comforting, whereas a humorous person radiates a general pleasure and is like another candle in the room.

30. According to the author, a humorous person is like

(A) an expensive gift
(B) a loaded gun
(C) an unusual puppet
(D) a comforting light
(E) a mechanical toy

31. The author uses the analogy of marionettes to illustrate that humorous people

(A) are never forgotten
(B) smile frequently
(C) control their companions
(D) surprise their friends
(E) attract many friends

32. The author implies that witty people are likely to make remarks that are

(A) sentimental
(B) emotional
(C) displeasing
(D) irrelevant
(E) explanatory

33. Which of the following best expresses the author's main point?

(A) It is more pleasant to be with humorous people than with witty people.
(B) Humor is more difficult to achieve than wit.
(C) Humorous people make friends easily.
(D) Humor and wit are genuine gifts.
(E) Witty people are not usually humorous, but humorous people are usually witty.

GO ON TO THE NEXT PAGE.

Improvements in technology, in the tools and crafts men employ in making a living, have too often been ignored by the historical annalist. Farmers, carpenters, and miners live on a different level from philosophers, poets, and historians; the invention of the wheelbarrow, the windmill, and the horse collar were innovations of little interest

Line 5 to scholars on their high, intellectual plateau. This gulf between theory and practice, between those who labor and those who think, has perverted the writing of history, giving it a one-sided, intellectualized interpretation. The humanists, for instance, when they peered backward from the fifteenth century, concluded that the thousand years following the collapse of Roman rule had been a dark age. It seemed so to them because

10 arts and letters and other manifestations of the high intellectual tradition had declined when the Roman Empire in the West disintegrated and had not revived until their own day.

Had the humanists paid more attention to technological developments, they might have modified their conception of the "dark ages," for the practical inventive

15 genius of the European peoples continued to function although the Roman Empire dissolved. Medieval craftsmen devised and introduced labor-saving devices which even the Greeks and Romans had failed to invent when their civilization was flourishing so brilliantly in the thousand years between 600 BCE and 400 CE. In some respects medieval society was neither static nor stagnant despite the contempt the humanists conceived for it.

34. Which of the following is the author's main point?
   (A) It is impossible ever to bridge the gulf between scientists and humanists.
   (B) Medieval society was intellectually inferior to that of the preceding Roman Empire.
   (C) The writing of history should emphasize intellectual activities rather than technological developments.
   (D) It is possible for historians to present an inaccurate view of civilizations because of their intellectual bias.
   (E) The inventions of the Greeks and Romans provided the ideas for labor-saving devices of medieval times.

35. In the author's opinion, medieval civilization was superior to the Greek and Roman civilizations in the area of
   (A) painting
   (B) philosophy
   (C) technology
   (D) government
   (E) the writing of history

36. According to the author, the fifteenth-century humanists considered the preceding thousand years to be a "dark age" (line 14) because
   (A) intellectual accomplishments did not flourish
   (B) labor-saving devices had not yet been invented
   (C) the level of technological development was so low
   (D) the years prior to Roman rule had been so brilliant
   (E) the laborers and the philosophers could not communicate with one another

37. The author apparently believes that historical accounts would be more accurate if
   (A) history was written solely for humanists
   (B) technology was subordinated to philosophy
   (C) historians were required to define their terms
   (D) technological developments were not ignored
   (E) intellectual endeavors were taken into account

GO ON TO THE NEXT PAGE.

I have seen a baby canary two days out of the nest take a bath in the water where I had been soaking seeds, and a thorough job he did of it, too! Once finished, he dried his face by wiping it, his tail by shaking it, and his wings by picking the drops of water with his bill. You could hardly believe it, even though you knew it was just his ghostly,

Line 5   departed relatives working through him.

38. Which of the following is probably true of the young canary?

(A) He knew how to bathe by instinct.
(B) He took his first bath entirely by accident.
(C) He was a figment of the writer's imagination.
(D) He was introduced to the water by the writer.
(E) He had taken several baths before the writer saw him.

39. The writer's reaction to watching the young canary take a bath is one of

(A) reverence
(B) sympathy
(C) amazement
(D) amusement
(E) indifference

40. What does the author mean when he says, "it was just his ghostly, departed relatives working through him" (lines 4-5)?

(A) The canary's relatives looked after him while he bathed.
(B) The bird was taught how to take a bath before he left the nest.
(C) Even though the canary's mother had left, she was still watching over him.
(D) The canary was taking a bath more out of fear than a desire to be clean.
(E) The canary was acting according to his inherited ability to take care of himself.

STOP
**IF YOU FINISH BEFORE TIME IS CALLED,
YOU MAY CHECK YOUR WORK ON THIS SECTION ONLY.
DO NOT TURN TO ANY OTHER SECTION IN THE TEST.**

SECTION 3
60 Questions

This section consists of two different types of questions: synonyms and analogies. There are directions and a sample question for each type.

Synonyms
Each of the following questions consists of one word followed by five words or phrases. You are to select the one word or phrase whose meaning is closest to the word in capital letters.

Sample Question:

> CHILLY:
>
> (A) lazy
> (B) nice
> (C) dry
> (D) cold
> (E) sunny
>
> Ⓐ Ⓑ Ⓒ ● Ⓔ

1. COLLABORATE:
   (A) settle
   (B) embroider
   (C) forge ahead
   (D) pass sentence
   (E) work together

2. AILMENT:
   (A) illness
   (B) arrival
   (C) affection
   (D) ignorance
   (E) enthusiasm

3. MEMENTO:
   (A) script
   (B) badge
   (C) souvenir
   (D) directory
   (E) engraving

4. JEOPARDIZE:
   (A) liberate
   (B) improvise
   (C) endanger
   (D) simonize
   (E) implicate

5. FIASCO:
   (A) regret
   (B) calculation
   (C) inexperience
   (D) total failure
   (E) thorough dejection

6. COLOSSAL:
   (A) limp
   (B) huge
   (C) close
   (D) sweet
   (E) smooth

7. FLAMBOYANT:
   (A) showy
   (B) certain
   (C) aggressive
   (D) independent
   (E) accommodating

8. EMPATHY:
   (A) pathos
   (B) apathy
   (C) telepathy
   (D) forcefulness
   (E) understanding

GO ON TO THE NEXT PAGE.

9. EXHILARATE:
   (A) expel
   (B) repeat
   (C) excite
   (D) discuss
   (E) display

10. ENCUMBER:
    (A) repel
    (B) burden
    (C) agitate
    (D) disprove
    (E) disappoint

11. JEER:
    (A) avoid
    (B) desert
    (C) call for
    (D) scoff at
    (E) take from

12. RETORT:
    (A) sharp answer
    (B) naive question
    (C) deafening shout
    (D) arrogant demand
    (E) careless error

13. MEDLEY:
    (A) mood
    (B) motive
    (C) mixture
    (D) mastery
    (E) measure

14. DUBIOUS:
    (A) useful
    (B) devious
    (C) honest
    (D) doubtful
    (E) synchronous

15. CALLOW:
    (A) small
    (B) elderly
    (C) unseen
    (D) wooden
    (E) unsophisticated

16. INSTIGATE:
    (A) do without
    (B) stir up
    (C) cry out
    (D) try again
    (E) go along

17. DEBILITATED:
    (A) charged
    (B) released
    (C) annoyed
    (D) weakened
    (E) intolerant

18. IDIOSYNCRASY:
    (A) inquiring attitude
    (B) illogical conclusion
    (C) instinctive reaction
    (D) impressive cunning
    (E) individual peculiarity

19. SIMULATE:
    (A) pause
    (B) hinder
    (C) reform
    (D) include
    (E) pretend

20. LORE:
    (A) sound judgment
    (B) undivided attention
    (C) organized resistance
    (D) traditional knowledge
    (E) complicated arrangement

GO ON TO THE NEXT PAGE.

21. CULTIVATE:

   (A) create
   (B) nurture
   (C) activate
   (D) neglect
   (E) landscape

22. QUALM:

   (A) decree
   (B) captivity
   (C) violation
   (D) misgiving
   (E) obligation

23. TENTATIVE:

   (A) hurried
   (B) enticing
   (C) uncertain
   (D) excited
   (E) thoughtless

24. PRECOCIOUS:

   (A) quick
   (B) erratic
   (C) valuable
   (D) advanced
   (E) dangerous

25. BURGEON:

   (A) profit
   (B) debase
   (C) flourish
   (D) extract
   (E) galvanize

26. ACUMEN:

   (A) humor
   (B) malice
   (C) intellect
   (D) ignorance
   (E) optimism

27. IMPRUDENT:

   (A) irritated
   (B) sluggish
   (C) awkward
   (D) foolhardy
   (E) incoherent

28. ABORIGINAL:

   (A) unique
   (B) hateful
   (C) flexible
   (D) essential
   (E) primordial

29. BRANDISH:

   (A) burn
   (B) mark
   (C) boast
   (D) wave
   (E) quarrel

30. RAZE:

   (A) clutter
   (B) unhook
   (C) demolish
   (D) minimize
   (E) counteract

GO ON TO THE NEXT PAGE.

Analogies

The following questions ask you to find relationships between words. For each question, select the answer choice that best completes the meaning of the sentence.

Sample Question:

> Kitten is to cat as
> (A) fawn is to colt
> (B) puppy is to dog
> (C) cow is to bull
> (D) wolf is to bear
> (E) hen is to rooster

Choice (B) is the best answer because a kitten is a young cat just as a puppy is a young dog. Of all the answer choices, (B) states a relationship that is most like the relationship between <u>kitten</u> and <u>cat</u>.

---

31. Menu is to foods as

    (A) sign is to roads
    (B) digest is to stories
    (C) magazine is to editions
    (D) catalog is to merchandise
    (E) encyclopedia is to volumes

32. Milk is to butter as

    (A) jelly is to bread
    (B) shirt is to clothes
    (C) wood is to paper
    (D) factory is to mill
    (E) vegetable is to colander

33. Photography is to images as

    (A) painting is to talent
    (B) sculpture is to forms
    (C) knitting is to dexterity
    (D) caricature is to etchings
    (E) statistics is to mathematics

34. Eternity is to time as

    (A) deity is to religion
    (B) credulity is to love
    (C) infinity is to number
    (D) community is to size
    (E) maternity is to motherhood

35. Teacher is to assignment as doctor is to

    (A) disease
    (B) hospital
    (C) operation
    (D) stethoscope
    (E) prescription

36. Farmer is to cook as

    (A) barber is to tailor
    (B) rancher is to miner
    (C) physician is to dentist
    (D) plumber is to electrician
    (E) lumberjack is to carpenter

37. Creep is to run as

    (A) fall is to dive
    (B) trickle is to pour
    (C) shift is to change
    (D) anchor is to moor
    (E) recoil is to bounce

38. Copious is to abundant as docile is to

    (A) bulk
    (B) meek
    (C) temper
    (D) dominant
    (E) momentous

GO ON TO THE NEXT PAGE.

39. Calendar is to days as
    (A) caliper is to density
    (B) odometer is to aroma
    (C) sundial is to sunlight
    (D) fluoroscope is to light
    (E) chronometer is to time

40. Avarice is to greed as
    (A) fury is to anger
    (B) stream is to pond
    (C) flurries is to blizzard
    (D) insight is to epiphany
    (E) laughter is to delight

41. Shelter is to protection as
    (A) pane is to window
    (B) bed is to blanket
    (C) picture is to wall
    (D) curtain is to privacy
    (E) lampshade is to brightness

42. Evict is to home as
    (A) bewitch is to magic
    (B) conjure is to amulet
    (C) possess is to treasure
    (D) banish is to country
    (E) charm is to location

43. Paroled is to pardoned as conditional is to
    (A) absolute
    (B) corrupted
    (C) improbable
    (D) annihilated
    (E) manipulated

44. Nonfiction is to biography as fiction is to
    (A) essay
    (B) history
    (C) novel
    (D) editorial
    (E) autobiography

45. Capitulate is to surrender as
    (A) insinuate is to pause
    (B) prevaricate is to flatter
    (C) remonstrate is to protest
    (D) attenuate is to strengthen
    (E) amalgamate is to separate

46. Contract is to individuals as
    (A) treaty is to nations
    (B) license is to permits
    (C) cohesion is to unions
    (D) marriage is to proposal
    (E) alliance is to permanence

47. Prune is to eradicate as
    (A) write is to edit
    (B) infer is to criticize
    (C) abbreviate is to delete
    (D) condense is to abridge
    (E) assume is to conclude

48. Discovering is to cache as
    (A) overlooking is to fact
    (B) overhearing is to secret
    (C) overhauling is to engine
    (D) overpaying is to employee
    (E) overthrowing is to government

49. Glare is to light as
    (A) stare is to vision
    (B) blaze is to smoke
    (C) blare is to sound
    (D) power is to steam
    (E) motion is to speed

50. Competent is to worker as
    (A) pleasant is to artist
    (B) bright is to dancer
    (C) fluent is to speaker
    (D) dignified is to general
    (E) orderly is to professor

GO ON TO THE NEXT PAGE.

51. Paint is to corrosion as grease is to
    (A) friction
    (B) flotation
    (C) rotation
    (D) contraction
    (E) combustion

52. Stoicism is to endurance as
    (A) awe is to astonishment
    (B) inspiration is to expiration
    (C) commitment is to despair
    (D) resolution is to anger
    (E) primary is to secondary

53. Hinge is to door as
    (A) ink is to pen
    (B) lock is to key
    (C) bulb is to lamp
    (D) bell is to tower
    (E) fulcrum is to lever

54. Song is to playlist as
    (A) verse is to prose
    (B) ditty is to sonnet
    (C) art is to museum
    (D) trumpet is to brass
    (E) poem is to anthology

55. Consume is to devour as
    (A) warn is to alert
    (B) shove is to push
    (C) pursue is to follow
    (D) suspend is to expel
    (E) upset is to annoy

56. Drizzle is to downpour as
    (A) rain is to trickle
    (B) storm is to drought
    (C) kindle is to blaze
    (D) minute is to hour
    (E) primary is to secondary

57. Flowery is to prose as
    (A) realistic is to film
    (B) obscene is to humor
    (C) rhythmic is to music
    (D) ornate is to furniture
    (E) historical is to uniform

58. Contort is to straighten as
    (A) twist is to shout
    (B) devour is to eat
    (C) obscure is to darken
    (D) entangle is to streamline
    (E) complicate is to obfuscate

59. Commission is to appointment as
    (A) mission is to trip
    (B) emission is to car
    (C) fission is to science
    (D) admission is to ticket
    (E) intermission is to break

60. Autograph is to pen as
    (A) calf is to cow
    (B) bait is to lure
    (C) danger is to harm
    (D) data is to calculator
    (E) thermometer is to temperature

STOP
**IF YOU FINISH BEFORE TIME IS CALLED,
YOU MAY CHECK YOUR WORK ON THIS SECTION ONLY.
DO NOT TURN TO ANY OTHER SECTION IN THE TEST.**

SECTION 4
25 Questions

Following each problem in this section, there are five suggested answers. Work each problem in your head or in the blank space provided at the right of the page. Then look at the five suggested answers and decide which one is best.

<u>Note:</u> Figures that accompany problems in this section are drawn as accurately as possible EXCEPT when it is stated in a specific problem that its figure is not drawn to scale.

Sample Problem:

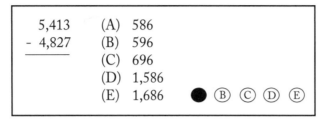

USE THIS SPACE FOR FIGURING.

1. Two numbers whose difference is 8 add up to 50. Identify the smaller number.
   - (A) 21
   - (B) 22
   - (C) 23
   - (D) 28
   - (E) 29

2. If $50 \times A = 50$, then $50 - A =$
   - (A) 0
   - (B) $\frac{1}{50}$
   - (C) 1
   - (D) 51
   - (E) 49

3. $200 - 7\frac{15}{16} =$
   - (A) $192\frac{1}{16}$
   - (B) $192\frac{15}{16}$
   - (C) $193\frac{1}{4}$
   - (D) $193\frac{15}{16}$
   - (E) 194

GO ON TO THE NEXT PAGE.

USE THIS SPACE FOR FIGURING.

4. A rope $7\frac{1}{4}$ feet long can be cut into how many pieces each 3 inches long?

    (A) 8
    (B) 15
    (C) 21
    (D) 22
    (E) 29

5. $0.040 \times 100.00 =$

    (A) 0.04
    (B) 0.4
    (C) 4.0
    (D) 40
    (E) 400

6. If $X > 4$, then $3X + 6$ could be

    (A) 15
    (B) 16
    (C) 17
    (D) 18
    (E) 19

7. Find the quotient of 6.2 and 0.31.

    (A) $\frac{1}{20}$
    (B) $\frac{1}{2}$
    (C) 2
    (D) 20
    (E) 200

8. The average height of two boys is 5.2 feet and the average height of four girls is 4.9 feet. What is the average height, in feet, of all six children?

    (A) 3.83
    (B) 4.8
    (C) 4.9
    (D) 5
    (E) 5.05

GO ON TO THE NEXT PAGE.

USE THIS SPACE FOR FIGURING.

9. All of the following products are equal EXCEPT

(A) $1 \times \frac{1}{4}$

(B) $2 \times \frac{1}{8}$

(C) $4 \times \frac{1}{16}$

(D) $5 \times \frac{1}{20}$

(E) $6 \times \frac{10}{24}$

10. What is the value of the greatest of four consecutive integers if the least minus twice the greatest equals 8?

(A) –14

(B) –11

(C) –2

(D) 1

(E) 4

Questions 11-12 refer to the graph.

11. What fraction of the Taylors' monthly income is spent for food?

(A) $\frac{1}{10}$

(B) $\frac{3}{20}$

(C) $\frac{1}{5}$

(D) $\frac{1}{4}$

(E) $\frac{3}{10}$

12. The amount the Taylors spend for taxes, Social Security, and pensions is what percent of the amount they spend for house payments, heat, and electricity?

(A) 30%

(B) 50%

(C) 60%

(D) 80%

(E) 90%

HOW THE TAYLORS SPEND THEIR MONTHLY INCOME

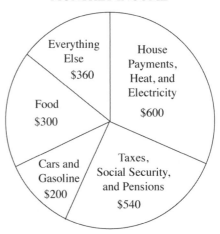

13. Mr. Kocher paid $30,000 for a rectangular lot 1,200 feet wide and 1,600 feet long. What was his approximate cost per square foot?

(A) 1.6¢

(B) 16¢

(C) $1.60

(D) $6.10

(E) $16.00

GO ON TO THE NEXT PAGE.

USE THIS SPACE FOR FIGURING.

14. One staple weighs 31 mg. If a box of staples holds 250 staples, how many grams does the whole box of staples weigh?

(A) 6.75
(B) 7.75
(C) 67.5
(D) 77.5
(E) 7,750

15. A truck driver took between $5\frac{1}{2}$ and 6 hours to make a 350-mile trip. The average speed, in miles per hour, must have been between

(A) 48 and 50
(B) 50 and 55
(C) 55 and 58
(D) 59 and 63
(E) 64 and 100

16. $\dfrac{4x^{-3}z}{2^{-2}y^4w^{-2}} =$

(A) $\dfrac{2y^4z}{x^{-3}w^{-2}}$

(B) $\dfrac{2z}{x^3y^4w^2}$

(C) $\dfrac{8w^2z}{x^3y^4}$

(D) $\dfrac{16w^2z}{x^3y^4}$

(E) $\dfrac{w^2z}{x^3y^4}$

17. $6\overline{)936} =$

(A) $\dfrac{900}{6} \times \dfrac{30}{6} \times \dfrac{6}{6}$

(B) $\dfrac{900}{6} + \dfrac{30}{6} + \dfrac{6}{6}$

(C) $\dfrac{90}{6} + \dfrac{36}{6}$

(D) $\dfrac{900}{6} + 36$

(E) $\dfrac{9}{6} + \dfrac{3}{6} + \dfrac{6}{6}$

GO ON TO THE NEXT PAGE.

USE THIS SPACE FOR FIGURING.

18. Combine and simplify:

$(5x^3 + 7x - 3) - (x^3 - 2x^2 + 7x - 8)$

(A) $4x^3 - 2x^2 + 14x - 11$

(B) $4x^3 - 2x^2 - 11$

(C) $4x^3 + 2x^2 - 14x + 5$

(D) $4x^3 + 2x^2 - 11$

(E) $4x^3 + 2x^2 + 5$

19. Which of the following gives the number of cents in a dimes, n nickels, and 2 quarters?

(A) $\frac{a}{10} + \frac{n}{5} + 50$

(B) $\frac{10}{a} + \frac{5}{n} + 50$

(C) $a + 10n + 2$

(D) $10a + 5n + 50$

(E) $10a + 50n + 5$

20. In the figure, C is the center of the circle and $\angle ACB$ is right. Vertices A and B of the triangle are on the circle. If the area of the triangle ACB is 8, then what is the area of the shaded region?

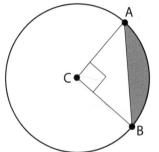

(A) $8 - 4\pi$

(B) $4\pi - 8$

(C) $16\pi - 8$

(D) $8\pi - 8$

(E) It cannot be determined from the information given.

21. A rectangular prism has a volume of 288 cubic meters. What are its dimensions?

(A) 12m by 6m by 2m

(B) 12m by 12m by 4m

(C) 8m by 8m by 4m

(D) 8m by 9m by 4m

(E) 4m by 7m by 9m

GO ON TO THE NEXT PAGE.

USE THIS SPACE FOR FIGURING.

22. Simplify the variable expression: $\dfrac{15g^2v^3z}{35gv^2z}$

    (A) $\dfrac{gv}{3}$

    (B) $\dfrac{3}{7gv}$

    (C) $\dfrac{3gv}{7}$

    (D) $\dfrac{3g^3v^5z^2}{7}$

    (E) $\dfrac{5gv}{7z}$

23. In a survey, each of 500 people was found to have a checking account, a savings account, or both. If 300 of these people have checking accounts and 300 have savings accounts, how many people have both a checking account and a savings account?

    (A) 50

    (B) 100

    (C) 150

    (D) 250

    (E) 300

24. Grandma's Soup Company packages tomato soup that serves four in cylindrical cans having a base diameter of 8 cm and a height of 10 cm. It wants to introduce the soup in single-serving cans as well. If the company keeps the height of the new can at 10 cm, what should its new base diameter equal?

    (A) 1

    (B) $\sqrt{2}$

    (C) 2

    (D) 4

    (E) $2\sqrt{2}$

25. If $a > 1$, which of the following is greatest?

    (A) $3a + 1$

    (B) $a + 1$

    (C) $a - 1$

    (D) $\dfrac{a}{a} + 1$

    (E) $a + \dfrac{1}{a}$

STOP
**IF YOU FINISH BEFORE TIME IS CALLED,
YOU MAY CHECK YOUR WORK ON THIS SECTION ONLY.
DO NOT TURN TO ANY OTHER SECTION IN THE TEST.**

THIS PAGE INTENTIONALLY LEFT BLANK.

Practice Test II: Upper Level Answer Sheet

Be sure each mark completely fills the answer space.
Start with number 1 for each new section of the test. You may find more answer spaces than you need.
If so, please leave them blank.

Section 1

1 Ⓐ Ⓑ Ⓒ Ⓓ Ⓔ	6 Ⓐ Ⓑ Ⓒ Ⓓ Ⓔ	11 Ⓐ Ⓑ Ⓒ Ⓓ Ⓔ	16 Ⓐ Ⓑ Ⓒ Ⓓ Ⓔ	21 Ⓐ Ⓑ Ⓒ Ⓓ Ⓔ
2 Ⓐ Ⓑ Ⓒ Ⓓ Ⓔ	7 Ⓐ Ⓑ Ⓒ Ⓓ Ⓔ	12 Ⓐ Ⓑ Ⓒ Ⓓ Ⓔ	17 Ⓐ Ⓑ Ⓒ Ⓓ Ⓔ	22 Ⓐ Ⓑ Ⓒ Ⓓ Ⓔ
3 Ⓐ Ⓑ Ⓒ Ⓓ Ⓔ	8 Ⓐ Ⓑ Ⓒ Ⓓ Ⓔ	13 Ⓐ Ⓑ Ⓒ Ⓓ Ⓔ	18 Ⓐ Ⓑ Ⓒ Ⓓ Ⓔ	23 Ⓐ Ⓑ Ⓒ Ⓓ Ⓔ
4 Ⓐ Ⓑ Ⓒ Ⓓ Ⓔ	9 Ⓐ Ⓑ Ⓒ Ⓓ Ⓔ	14 Ⓐ Ⓑ Ⓒ Ⓓ Ⓔ	19 Ⓐ Ⓑ Ⓒ Ⓓ Ⓔ	24 Ⓐ Ⓑ Ⓒ Ⓓ Ⓔ
5 Ⓐ Ⓑ Ⓒ Ⓓ Ⓔ	10 Ⓐ Ⓑ Ⓒ Ⓓ Ⓔ	15 Ⓐ Ⓑ Ⓒ Ⓓ Ⓔ	20 Ⓐ Ⓑ Ⓒ Ⓓ Ⓔ	25 Ⓐ Ⓑ Ⓒ Ⓓ Ⓔ

Section 2

1 Ⓐ Ⓑ Ⓒ Ⓓ Ⓔ	9 Ⓐ Ⓑ Ⓒ Ⓓ Ⓔ	17 Ⓐ Ⓑ Ⓒ Ⓓ Ⓔ	25 Ⓐ Ⓑ Ⓒ Ⓓ Ⓔ	33 Ⓐ Ⓑ Ⓒ Ⓓ Ⓔ
2 Ⓐ Ⓑ Ⓒ Ⓓ Ⓔ	10 Ⓐ Ⓑ Ⓒ Ⓓ Ⓔ	18 Ⓐ Ⓑ Ⓒ Ⓓ Ⓔ	26 Ⓐ Ⓑ Ⓒ Ⓓ Ⓔ	34 Ⓐ Ⓑ Ⓒ Ⓓ Ⓔ
3 Ⓐ Ⓑ Ⓒ Ⓓ Ⓔ	11 Ⓐ Ⓑ Ⓒ Ⓓ Ⓔ	19 Ⓐ Ⓑ Ⓒ Ⓓ Ⓔ	27 Ⓐ Ⓑ Ⓒ Ⓓ Ⓔ	35 Ⓐ Ⓑ Ⓒ Ⓓ Ⓔ
4 Ⓐ Ⓑ Ⓒ Ⓓ Ⓔ	12 Ⓐ Ⓑ Ⓒ Ⓓ Ⓔ	20 Ⓐ Ⓑ Ⓒ Ⓓ Ⓔ	28 Ⓐ Ⓑ Ⓒ Ⓓ Ⓔ	36 Ⓐ Ⓑ Ⓒ Ⓓ Ⓔ
5 Ⓐ Ⓑ Ⓒ Ⓓ Ⓔ	13 Ⓐ Ⓑ Ⓒ Ⓓ Ⓔ	21 Ⓐ Ⓑ Ⓒ Ⓓ Ⓔ	29 Ⓐ Ⓑ Ⓒ Ⓓ Ⓔ	37 Ⓐ Ⓑ Ⓒ Ⓓ Ⓔ
6 Ⓐ Ⓑ Ⓒ Ⓓ Ⓔ	14 Ⓐ Ⓑ Ⓒ Ⓓ Ⓔ	22 Ⓐ Ⓑ Ⓒ Ⓓ Ⓔ	30 Ⓐ Ⓑ Ⓒ Ⓓ Ⓔ	38 Ⓐ Ⓑ Ⓒ Ⓓ Ⓔ
7 Ⓐ Ⓑ Ⓒ Ⓓ Ⓔ	15 Ⓐ Ⓑ Ⓒ Ⓓ Ⓔ	23 Ⓐ Ⓑ Ⓒ Ⓓ Ⓔ	31 Ⓐ Ⓑ Ⓒ Ⓓ Ⓔ	39 Ⓐ Ⓑ Ⓒ Ⓓ Ⓔ
8 Ⓐ Ⓑ Ⓒ Ⓓ Ⓔ	16 Ⓐ Ⓑ Ⓒ Ⓓ Ⓔ	24 Ⓐ Ⓑ Ⓒ Ⓓ Ⓔ	32 Ⓐ Ⓑ Ⓒ Ⓓ Ⓔ	40 Ⓐ Ⓑ Ⓒ Ⓓ Ⓔ

Section 3

1 Ⓐ Ⓑ Ⓒ Ⓓ Ⓔ	13 Ⓐ Ⓑ Ⓒ Ⓓ Ⓔ	25 Ⓐ Ⓑ Ⓒ Ⓓ Ⓔ	37 Ⓐ Ⓑ Ⓒ Ⓓ Ⓔ	49 Ⓐ Ⓑ Ⓒ Ⓓ Ⓔ
2 Ⓐ Ⓑ Ⓒ Ⓓ Ⓔ	14 Ⓐ Ⓑ Ⓒ Ⓓ Ⓔ	26 Ⓐ Ⓑ Ⓒ Ⓓ Ⓔ	38 Ⓐ Ⓑ Ⓒ Ⓓ Ⓔ	50 Ⓐ Ⓑ Ⓒ Ⓓ Ⓔ
3 Ⓐ Ⓑ Ⓒ Ⓓ Ⓔ	15 Ⓐ Ⓑ Ⓒ Ⓓ Ⓔ	27 Ⓐ Ⓑ Ⓒ Ⓓ Ⓔ	39 Ⓐ Ⓑ Ⓒ Ⓓ Ⓔ	51 Ⓐ Ⓑ Ⓒ Ⓓ Ⓔ
4 Ⓐ Ⓑ Ⓒ Ⓓ Ⓔ	16 Ⓐ Ⓑ Ⓒ Ⓓ Ⓔ	28 Ⓐ Ⓑ Ⓒ Ⓓ Ⓔ	40 Ⓐ Ⓑ Ⓒ Ⓓ Ⓔ	52 Ⓐ Ⓑ Ⓒ Ⓓ Ⓔ
5 Ⓐ Ⓑ Ⓒ Ⓓ Ⓔ	17 Ⓐ Ⓑ Ⓒ Ⓓ Ⓔ	29 Ⓐ Ⓑ Ⓒ Ⓓ Ⓔ	41 Ⓐ Ⓑ Ⓒ Ⓓ Ⓔ	53 Ⓐ Ⓑ Ⓒ Ⓓ Ⓔ
6 Ⓐ Ⓑ Ⓒ Ⓓ Ⓔ	18 Ⓐ Ⓑ Ⓒ Ⓓ Ⓔ	30 Ⓐ Ⓑ Ⓒ Ⓓ Ⓔ	42 Ⓐ Ⓑ Ⓒ Ⓓ Ⓔ	54 Ⓐ Ⓑ Ⓒ Ⓓ Ⓔ
7 Ⓐ Ⓑ Ⓒ Ⓓ Ⓔ	19 Ⓐ Ⓑ Ⓒ Ⓓ Ⓔ	31 Ⓐ Ⓑ Ⓒ Ⓓ Ⓔ	43 Ⓐ Ⓑ Ⓒ Ⓓ Ⓔ	55 Ⓐ Ⓑ Ⓒ Ⓓ Ⓔ
8 Ⓐ Ⓑ Ⓒ Ⓓ Ⓔ	20 Ⓐ Ⓑ Ⓒ Ⓓ Ⓔ	32 Ⓐ Ⓑ Ⓒ Ⓓ Ⓔ	44 Ⓐ Ⓑ Ⓒ Ⓓ Ⓔ	56 Ⓐ Ⓑ Ⓒ Ⓓ Ⓔ
9 Ⓐ Ⓑ Ⓒ Ⓓ Ⓔ	21 Ⓐ Ⓑ Ⓒ Ⓓ Ⓔ	33 Ⓐ Ⓑ Ⓒ Ⓓ Ⓔ	45 Ⓐ Ⓑ Ⓒ Ⓓ Ⓔ	57 Ⓐ Ⓑ Ⓒ Ⓓ Ⓔ
10 Ⓐ Ⓑ Ⓒ Ⓓ Ⓔ	22 Ⓐ Ⓑ Ⓒ Ⓓ Ⓔ	34 Ⓐ Ⓑ Ⓒ Ⓓ Ⓔ	46 Ⓐ Ⓑ Ⓒ Ⓓ Ⓔ	58 Ⓐ Ⓑ Ⓒ Ⓓ Ⓔ
11 Ⓐ Ⓑ Ⓒ Ⓓ Ⓔ	23 Ⓐ Ⓑ Ⓒ Ⓓ Ⓔ	35 Ⓐ Ⓑ Ⓒ Ⓓ Ⓔ	47 Ⓐ Ⓑ Ⓒ Ⓓ Ⓔ	59 Ⓐ Ⓑ Ⓒ Ⓓ Ⓔ
12 Ⓐ Ⓑ Ⓒ Ⓓ Ⓔ	24 Ⓐ Ⓑ Ⓒ Ⓓ Ⓔ	36 Ⓐ Ⓑ Ⓒ Ⓓ Ⓔ	48 Ⓐ Ⓑ Ⓒ Ⓓ Ⓔ	60 Ⓐ Ⓑ Ⓒ Ⓓ Ⓔ

Section 4

1 Ⓐ Ⓑ Ⓒ Ⓓ Ⓔ	6 Ⓐ Ⓑ Ⓒ Ⓓ Ⓔ	11 Ⓐ Ⓑ Ⓒ Ⓓ Ⓔ	16 Ⓐ Ⓑ Ⓒ Ⓓ Ⓔ	21 Ⓐ Ⓑ Ⓒ Ⓓ Ⓔ
2 Ⓐ Ⓑ Ⓒ Ⓓ Ⓔ	7 Ⓐ Ⓑ Ⓒ Ⓓ Ⓔ	12 Ⓐ Ⓑ Ⓒ Ⓓ Ⓔ	17 Ⓐ Ⓑ Ⓒ Ⓓ Ⓔ	22 Ⓐ Ⓑ Ⓒ Ⓓ Ⓔ
3 Ⓐ Ⓑ Ⓒ Ⓓ Ⓔ	8 Ⓐ Ⓑ Ⓒ Ⓓ Ⓔ	13 Ⓐ Ⓑ Ⓒ Ⓓ Ⓔ	18 Ⓐ Ⓑ Ⓒ Ⓓ Ⓔ	23 Ⓐ Ⓑ Ⓒ Ⓓ Ⓔ
4 Ⓐ Ⓑ Ⓒ Ⓓ Ⓔ	9 Ⓐ Ⓑ Ⓒ Ⓓ Ⓔ	14 Ⓐ Ⓑ Ⓒ Ⓓ Ⓔ	19 Ⓐ Ⓑ Ⓒ Ⓓ Ⓔ	24 Ⓐ Ⓑ Ⓒ Ⓓ Ⓔ
5 Ⓐ Ⓑ Ⓒ Ⓓ Ⓔ	10 Ⓐ Ⓑ Ⓒ Ⓓ Ⓔ	15 Ⓐ Ⓑ Ⓒ Ⓓ Ⓔ	20 Ⓐ Ⓑ Ⓒ Ⓓ Ⓔ	25 Ⓐ Ⓑ Ⓒ Ⓓ Ⓔ

Section 5

1 Ⓐ Ⓑ Ⓒ Ⓓ Ⓔ	5 Ⓐ Ⓑ Ⓒ Ⓓ Ⓔ	9 Ⓐ Ⓑ Ⓒ Ⓓ Ⓔ	13 Ⓐ Ⓑ Ⓒ Ⓓ Ⓔ
2 Ⓐ Ⓑ Ⓒ Ⓓ Ⓔ	6 Ⓐ Ⓑ Ⓒ Ⓓ Ⓔ	10 Ⓐ Ⓑ Ⓒ Ⓓ Ⓔ	14 Ⓐ Ⓑ Ⓒ Ⓓ Ⓔ
3 Ⓐ Ⓑ Ⓒ Ⓓ Ⓔ	7 Ⓐ Ⓑ Ⓒ Ⓓ Ⓔ	11 Ⓐ Ⓑ Ⓒ Ⓓ Ⓔ	15 Ⓐ Ⓑ Ⓒ Ⓓ Ⓔ
4 Ⓐ Ⓑ Ⓒ Ⓓ Ⓔ	8 Ⓐ Ⓑ Ⓒ Ⓓ Ⓔ	12 Ⓐ Ⓑ Ⓒ Ⓓ Ⓔ	16 Ⓐ Ⓑ Ⓒ Ⓓ Ⓔ

Experimental Section – See page 11 for details.

THIS PAGE INTENTIONALLY LEFT BLANK.

Writing Sample

Schools would like to get to know you better through an essay or story you write using one of the two topics below. Please select the topic you find most interesting and fill in the circle next to the topic you choose.

Ⓐ What is something that you think needs to be invented and why?

Ⓑ His hands shook as he tried to untie it.

Use this page and the next page to complete your writing sample.

Continue on next page.

SECTION 1
25 Questions

Following each problem in this section, there are five suggested answers. Work each problem in your head or in the blank space provided at the right of the page. Then look at the five suggested answers and decide which one is best.

<u>Note:</u> Figures that accompany problems in this section are drawn as accurately as possible EXCEPT when it is stated in a specific problem that its figure is not drawn to scale.

Sample Problem:

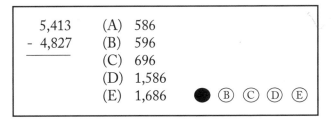

USE THIS SPACE FOR FIGURING.

1. Jen plans to give a chocolate bar to each of her 21 party guests. There are four chocolate bars in each package. How many packages must she buy?
   - (A) 4
   - (B) 5
   - (C) 6
   - (D) 7
   - (E) 10

2. Patrick has $250 in the bank. If he takes out 40%, how much money will he have left in the bank?
   - (A) $100
   - (B) $150
   - (C) $210
   - (D) $290
   - (E) $350

GO ON TO THE NEXT PAGE.

USE THIS SPACE FOR FIGURING.

3. In the figure, if b is a whole number, which of the following could be the length of segment PQ?

   (A) 7
   (B) 10
   (C) 14
   (D) 15
   (E) 16

4. In the figure, if the perimeters of quadrilateral region A and triangular region B are each equal to 27, then $x + y =$

   (A) 9
   (B) 12
   (C) 15
   (D) 18
   (E) 24

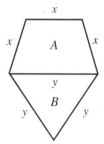

5. $\left(-\dfrac{5}{4}\right)^3 =$

   (A) $-\dfrac{125}{64}$

   (B) $-\dfrac{15}{12}$

   (C) $-\dfrac{15}{64}$

   (D) $\dfrac{15}{12}$

   (E) $\dfrac{125}{64}$

6. On the figure shown, point P will be located at the mid-point of side RS and point Q will be located at the midpoint of side ST. Which lettered point will be located at the midpoint of a line segment joining P and Q?

   (A) A
   (B) B
   (C) C
   (D) D
   (E) E

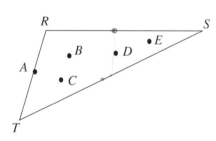

GO ON TO THE NEXT PAGE.

USE THIS SPACE FOR FIGURING.

7. Which of the following could be the value of X
    if $\frac{1}{4} + X > 1$?

    (A) $\frac{1}{2}$

    (B) $\frac{1}{3}$

    (C) $\frac{2}{3}$

    (D) $\frac{3}{5}$

    (E) $\frac{4}{5}$

8. According to the graph in the figure, on which day
    was there the greatest increase in the number of cars
    produced compared to the day before?

    (A) Monday
    (B) Tuesday
    (C) Wednesday
    (D) Thursday
    (E) Friday

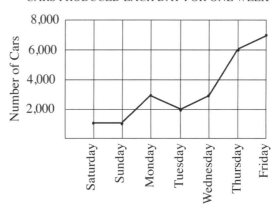

CARS PRODUCED EACH DAY FOR ONE WEEK

9. What is the measure of ∠ADC?

    (A) 60°
    (B) 85°
    (C) 95°
    (D) 120°
    (E) 145°

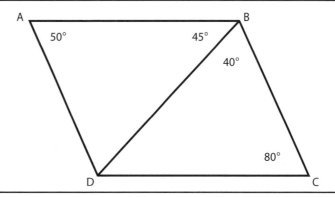

10. There are 15 boxes in a warehouse that need to be
    shipped by truck. If at least one but no more than five
    boxes must go in each truck and no two trucks can have
    the same number of boxes, what is the smallest number
    of trucks required to ship the 15 boxes?

    (A) 3
    (B) 4
    (C) 5
    (D) 10
    (E) 12

GO ON TO THE NEXT PAGE.

USE THIS SPACE FOR FIGURING.

11. When $T + S = 6$ and $2H + S = 6$, what is the value of H?

   (A) 12
   (B) 6
   (C) –6
   (D) –3
   (E) It cannot be determined from the information given.

12. The shaded region in the figure shown is divided by lines K, L, M, and S. The area between K and M is 45 square meters, between L and S is 40 square meters, and between M and S is 25 square meters. What is the area, in square meters, between K and L ?

   (A) 20
   (B) 30
   (C) 35
   (D) 60
   (E) 110

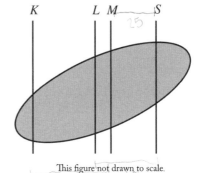

This figure not drawn to scale.

13. $\frac{79{,}865}{2{,}213}$ most closely equals which of the following?

   (A) 40
   (B) 4,000
   (C) 22,000
   (D) 36,000
   (E) 80,000

14. Omar begins training for a 5 km race by running 0.75 km the first day, 0.85 km the second day, and 0.95 km the third day. If he keeps increasing his distance each day according to the pace of his first three days, on what number day in his training program will Omar first run at least 5 km?

   (A) 42
   (B) 43
   (C) 44
   (D) 50
   (E) 500

GO ON TO THE NEXT PAGE.

USE THIS SPACE FOR FIGURING.

15. Johnny lives 20 miles from the deli and Hannah lives 12 miles from the same deli. In total miles, how far is Johnny's house from Hannah's house?

    (A) 8 miles
    (B) 14 miles
    (C) 32 miles
    (D) 40 miles
    (E) It cannot be determined from the information given.

16. If one third of the weight of a given truck is 2.4 tons, the weight of three trucks of the exact same weight as the given truck can be determined by multiplying 2.4 by which of the following?

    (A) $\frac{1}{3}$

    (B) $\frac{2}{3}$

    (C) $1\frac{1}{3}$

    (D) 3

    (E) 9

17. Which of the following must be true if two numbers, H and J, have an average of 100 and J is less than H?

    (A) $H - 100 = 100 - J$
    (B) $H = 100 + J$
    (C) $H + J = 100$
    (D) $H - J = 50$
    (E) $H = 100$ and $J = 100$

18. Which of the following could be the lengths of the sides of a triangle?

    (A) 3, 3, 6
    (B) 1, 2, 3
    (C) 3, 5, 6
    (D) 3, 5, 8
    (E) 8, 8, 19

GO ON TO THE NEXT PAGE.

USE THIS SPACE FOR FIGURING.

19. A store offers a 15% discount on all shoes. If a pair of shoes has an original price of $21.25, which of the following is closest to the price after the discount is taken?

(A) $17.50
(B) $18.00
(C) $18.50
(D) $19.00
(E) $19.50

20. The heights of a maple tree and a cherry tree have a ratio of 5:2. If the maple tree grew 20 cm and 20 cm was cut off the top of the cherry tree, the ratio of their heights would be 3:1. How much taller is the maple tree than the cherry tree?

(A) 240 cm
(B) 160 cm
(C) 400 cm
(D) 280 cm
(E) 260 cm

21. In the addition of the three-digit numbers shown, the letters A, B, C, and D each represent a unique single digit. Which of the following could be the sum of A + B + C + D?

(A) 10
(B) 13
(C) 14
(D) 16
(E) 19

$$\begin{array}{r} A\ B\ C \\ +\ D\ B\ C \\ \hline 8\ 5\ 0 \end{array}$$

22. If 90 percent of a is 44, what is 30 percent of $3a$?

(A) 30
(B) 44
(C) 45
(D) 49
(E) 90

GO ON TO THE NEXT PAGE.

USE THIS SPACE FOR FIGURING.

23. Each exterior angle of an equilateral triangle has which measure?

    (A) 60°
    (B) 120°
    (C) 180°
    (D) 240°
    (E) 360°

24. If the average of five consecutive whole numbers is 40, what is the smallest number?

    (A) 30
    (B) 35
    (C) 38
    (D) 40
    (E) 200

25. A hamburger stand has an average of 150 customers per day. To increase business, the owner plans to reduce the regular price of a burger from $5.00 to $4.00 before 5 p.m. each day. If 50 people pay $5.00, how many people must pay $4.00 if daily sales are to remain the same as before the $4.00 price reduction plan?

    (A) 100
    (B) 125
    (C) 130
    (D) 150
    (E) 200

STOP
**IF YOU FINISH BEFORE TIME IS CALLED,
YOU MAY CHECK YOUR WORK ON THIS SECTION ONLY.
DO NOT TURN TO ANY OTHER SECTION IN THE TEST.**

111

SECTION 2
40 Questions

Read each passage carefully and then answer the questions about it. For each question, decide on the basis of the passage which one of the choices best answers the question.

> Chopin's own playing was the counterpart of his personality. Every characteristic that could be distinguished in the man was apparent in the pianist—the same precision; the horror of excess and all that is careless and uncontrolled; the same good manners and high tone of character, combined with poetic warmth and a romantic fervor of
>
> *Line 5* expression. No one had ever heard such polished playing, although others could make a more overwhelming impression by their rush and violence. It is a mistake, encouraged by sentimental legend, to believe that Chopin's playing was limited by a delicacy which was equivalent to weakness. Even in the last stages of tuberculosis, he could rally and play with an energy that surprised the audience, who saw in front of them "a slight,
>
> *10* frail-looking person." At his final public appearance in November 1848, less than a year before the end, he managed to play "with his usual brilliance."

1. Although he performed while seriously ill with tuberculosis, Chopin surprised the audience with his

    (A) frail appearance
    (B) polish
    (C) loss of control
    (D) violence
    (E) energetic playing

2. The "end" mentioned in line 11 most likely refers to

    (A) Chopin's retirement from public life
    (B) the decline of Chopin's genius
    (C) the invalidism caused by his illness
    (D) Chopin's death in 1849
    (E) the end of the concert tour

3. This passage deals primarily with Chopin's

    (A) musical compositions
    (B) musical performance
    (C) debilitating illness
    (D) aristocratic personality
    (E) romantic fervor

4. When discussing Chopin, the author's tone in the passage could best be described as

    (A) admiring
    (B) brusque
    (C) ironic
    (D) hesitant
    (E) anguished

GO ON TO THE NEXT PAGE.

As earth whirls along its endless journey through space, it has a companion that is always beside it—the moon. The moon is a small planet. It is only about one-fourth as big as the earth.

The moon is our nearest neighbor in space. The stars are billions of miles away.
Line 5 The sun is millions of miles away. But the moon is only about 239,000 miles away. That makes the moon truly a next-door neighbor.

In a way, the moon "belongs" to the earth. Just as earth moves around the sun, the moon moves around the earth. It is held in place by the tug of earth's stronger gravity. A planet that is held by another planet this way is called a satellite. The moon is earth's
10 satellite.

The moon is a ball of gray rock, some of which is covered with dust. It has no air or water—and, of course, no plants or animals. Its whole surface is nothing but mountains and plains of rock. When we look up at a full moon, we often see dark patches. These dark patches are the lowlands. They seem to form a shadowy face that
15 people have named "the man in the moon." The brighter parts of the moon are the highlands.

In ancient times, many people worshipped the moon. The Romans, who thought the moon was a goddess, named it Luna. Our word lunar means "of the moon."

5. Why does the author think that the moon "belongs" (line 7) to the earth?

(A) The moon could not exist without the earth.
(B) One can see the man in the moon from earth.
(C) Ancient Romans considered it a goddess.
(D) It is earth's nearest neighbor.
(E) It is a satellite of the earth.

6. Which of the following can be found on the moon?

(A) air
(B) water
(C) plants
(D) animals
(E) mountains

7. According to the author, which of the following most accounts for the "man in the moon?"

(A) a myth
(B) the lowlands
(C) a goddess
(D) the Romans
(E) the highlands

8. The author's main purpose for writing the passage is most likely to

(A) inform the reader about the moon
(B) dispel myths about the man in the moon
(C) describe the origin of the word "lunar"
(D) compare the moon and the earth
(E) explain why the ancient Romans worshipped the moon

9. According to the passage, which of the following statements is NOT true?

(A) The moon is a planet.
(B) The moon is a satellite.
(C) The moon's lowlands appear dark from the earth.
(D) The moon is four times larger than earth.
(E) The moon is closer to the earth than anything else in space.

GO ON TO THE NEXT PAGE.

Dinitrogen tetroxide is a chemical compound made up of nitrogen and oxygen. It is abbreviated N_2O_4 and is often simply called nitrogen tetroxide or NTO. Propelling rockets is one of the best examples of the use to which nitrogen tetroxide can be put. It is often combined with a hydrazine-based rocket fuel. Because it burns on contact

Line 5 without needing a separate source to ignite it, it is one of the most important rocket propellants ever developed.

By the late 1950s, NTO was the storable oxidizer of choice for U.S. and Soviet rockets. It was used on the space shuttle, and continues to be used on most geo-stationary satellites and many deep-space probes. However, its use is not without risk. NTO poisoning nearly killed three astronauts when dangerous fumes were vented inside their cabin by mistake.

10. It can be inferred that nitrogen tetroxide

(A) is expensive
(B) must be burned
(C) requires a license for use
(D) is vital to the space program
(E) should not be combined with any other substance

11. Which of the following titles best describes the content of the passage?

(A) Fire Prevention in Space
(B) A Chemical Experiment
(C) Why Nitrogen Tetroxide Is No Longer Used
(D) Nitrogen Tetroxide and the Soviets
(E) An Introduction to Nitrogen Tetroxide

12. The author suggests that nitrogen tetroxide

(A) is an illegal compound
(B) needs to be lit with fire
(C) must be carefully vented
(D) should be forbidden in space
(E) is only used for propelling rockets

13. The author uses the phrase "burns on contact" (line 4) to show that nitrogen tetroxide is

(A) very hot
(B) flammable
(C) useful in space
(D) used only with rocket fuel
(E) too dangerous to use in industry

14. According to the passage, nitrogen tetroxide

(A) cannot be stored
(B) has limited power
(C) is unusable at high altitudes
(D) is an important rocket propellant
(E) is not suitable for use in deep space

15. The author's tone in the second paragraph can best be described as

(A) bored
(B) serious
(C) annoyed
(D) humorous
(E) enthusiastic

GO ON TO THE NEXT PAGE.

Washington is full of green politicians supporting causes that other people demand they support. Indeed, this truism of human psychology is even truer of many so-called seasoned politicians. Like certain senators, many representatives, and all of the lobbyists, they portray themselves as VIPs, taking uncontroversial stances that capture

Line 5 the public's interest and pay off in the currency of fame.

But there is another, all too rare kind of politician: the authentic professional who steeps himself or herself in the art of public service with dazzling skill and persuasiveness. What marks these politicians, besides integrity, is their drive to achieve impressive results rather than fame, despite all the temptations of publicity and self-

10 indulgence. Most began their careers in local government, and for many, helping the little guy remains their top priority, despite the temptation to overlook the powerless. Above all, they seek to pose the unanswered questions—to make an honorable mark on an often false town.

16. The author is primarily concerned with
(A) defining politics
(B) criticizing artificial politicians
(C) praising politicians
(D) describing the historical role of the public servant
(E) considering the contributions politicians can make to society

17. The author admires politicians who
(A) enact meaningful change
(B) get a great deal of publicity
(C) overlook the local residents
(D) know how to enjoy themselves
(E) support only the most popular positions

18. The author would probably have the greatest respect for a politician who
(A) tackles meaningful issues
(B) attains international fame
(C) knows how to enjoy himself
(D) actively seeks the political limelight
(E) knows how to tell people what they want to hear

19. The author's attitude toward politicians who seek fame may best be described as
(A) sympathetic
(B) indifferent
(C) respectful
(D) amused
(E) critical

20. Which of the following is the author most likely to discuss next?
(A) how to relax and be yourself
(B) the glamour of a political career
(C) what makes certain politicians famous
(D) the careers of some exceptional politicians
(E) some of the most popular politicians today

GO ON TO THE NEXT PAGE.

We had a dreary morning's work before us, for there was no sign of any wind, and the boats had to be got out and manned, and the ship warped three or four miles round the corner of the island and up the narrow passage to the haven behind Skeleton Island. I volunteered for one of the boats, where I had, of course, no business. The heat was

Line 5 sweltering, and the men grumbled fiercely over their work. Anderson was in command of my boat, and instead of keeping the crew in order, he grumbled as loud as the worst.

"Well," he said with an oath, "it's not forever."

I thought this was a very bad sign, for up to that day the men had gone briskly and willingly about their business; but the very sight of the island had relaxed the cords

10 of discipline.

We brought up just where the anchor was in the char, about a third of a mile from each shore, the mainland on one side and Skeleton Island on the other. The bottom was clean sand. The plunge of our anchor sent up clouds of birds wheeling and crying over the woods, but in less than a minute they were down again and all was once more silent.

15 The place was entirely land-locked, buried in woods, the trees coming right down to high-water mark, the shores mostly flat, and the hilltops standing round at a distance in a sort of amphitheatre, one here, one there. From the ship we could see nothing of the house or stockade, for they were quite buried among trees; and if it had not been for the chart on the companion, we might have been the first that had ever anchored there

20 since the island arose out of the seas.

There was not a breath of air moving, nor a sound but that of the surf booming half a mile away along the beaches and against the rocks outside. A peculiar stagnant smell hung over the anchorage—a smell of sodden leaves and rotting tree trunks. I observed the doctor sniffing and sniffing, like someone tasting a bad egg.

25 "I don't know about treasure," he said, "but I'll stake my wig there's fever here."

If the conduct of the men had been alarming in the boat, it became truly threatening when they had come aboard. They lay about the deck growling together in talk. The slightest order was received with a black look and grudgingly and carelessly obeyed. Even the honest hands must have caught the infection, for there was not one man aboard to mend another. Mutiny it was plain, hung over us like a thunder-cloud.

21. The narrator of the passage is
    (A) in a lifeboat moving toward an island
    (B) in the captain's cabin, studying charts
    (C) on an island looking out toward the ocean
    (D) aboard a ship, scanning the distant horizon
    (E) aboard a ship, contemplating a nearby island

22. The mood of the crew is
    (A) sullen
    (B) relaxed
    (C) worried
    (D) perplexed
    (E) cooperative

23. The sensory image most important to this passage is
    (A) taste of a bad egg
    (B) sight of house and stockade
    (C) smell wafting from the island
    (D) sound of discontented sailors
    (E) sound of water lapping against the ship

24. The passage focuses on the
    (A) sense of ownership related to discovering a long-lost island
    (B) unexpected health hazards when at sea
    (C) pleasures of sailing on the open seas
    (D) uncertainty of running a sailing ship
    (E) dangers associated with hard labor

25. The passage is written from the viewpoint of which of the following?
    (A) the doctor
    (B) a crew member
    (C) an island dweller
    (D) the boat's commander
    (E) the captain of the ship

GO ON TO THE NEXT PAGE.

The National Black Theatre in Harlem is one of the great successes of our time. The survival of the institution and the way it has found a secure place in an increasingly crowded theater world are considerable accomplishments. Of greater significance, though, are the consistently high level of the institution's performances and the
Line 5 unfailing enthusiasm of each actor. Of all the theater groups that regularly appear in New York, it shows the least danger of succumbing to routine.

Dr. Barbara Ann Teer's National Black Theatre is animated by a sense of purpose that is largely moral in nature. In the midst of the despair that followed the 1968 assassination of Dr. Martin Luther King, Jr., Teer was determined to give American-
10 born actors of African descent a place on the stage. She sought to help other African-Americans so that they would not have to face the difficulties she had faced.

Nobody was better qualified than Teer to understand what black actors could do if given the incentive and the opportunity, and time has proved her faith well-founded. But Teer was too shrewd an artistic administrator and too serious an artist not to know
15 that the only standard she and her institution would in the long run be guided by is artistic. As she said in an interview, "We must begin building cultural centers where we can enjoy being free, open and black, where we can find out how talented we really are." That day, so far as I am concerned, has already arrived.

26. The author's primary purpose is to
   (A) describe how a theater institution is formed
   (B) discuss the success of one theater institution
   (C) contrast the artistic qualities of various theater institutions
   (D) encourage the establishment of more African American theater institutions
   (E) clarify the motives underlying the formation of theater institutions

27. Without changing the author's meaning, "secure" (line 2) could be replaced by
   (A) overconfident
   (B) profitable
   (C) shielded
   (D) assured
   (E) orderly

28. The author's attitude toward National Black Theatre can best be described as one of
   (A) cautious optimism
   (B) impulsive criticism
   (C) enthusiastic approval
   (D) theoretical justification
   (E) perplexed bewilderment

29. The author implies which of the following about theater institutions?
   (A) At present it is not possible to form new theater institutions.
   (B) Not all theater institutions survive against their competitors.
   (C) Most theater institutions regularly appear in New York City.
   (D) Most theater institutions maintain high levels of performance.
   (E) The best actors do not remain with the institutions that gave them their start.

30. Teer's attitude toward the artistic standards that should be used in judging the National Black Theatre is
   (A) unselfish
   (B) objective
   (C) simplistic
   (D) regrettable
   (E) noncommittal

GO ON TO THE NEXT PAGE.

Moses and his son Aaron may have been the first diviners when they used "the rod" to locate and bring forth water. In *The Odyssey*, the poet Homer refers to this practice as "rhabdomancy," Greek for "divining rod." Outside of biblical and ancient accounts, the first historical reference to divining is medieval. In Germany during the 1400s, divining

Line 5 devices were used extensively by miners seeking gold and silver and mineral ore.

Today, thousands of people still practice divining, following a method that is not much different from the one employed by those medieval miners. These diviners employ a hand-held instrument such as a forked stick, a pendulum bob on a string, an L-shaped metal rod, or a wooden wand to locate water, metal ores, or other valuables hidden

10 beneath the earth's surface. This rod is held firmly in the palms of the diviner's hands, and any sudden swing, either upward or downward, is taken as a signal of the presence of underground water, metal deposits, or even buried treasure. There are still questions as to whether or not this actually works, but there is no question that it is a popular practice throughout the world.

15 Skeptics point out that studies have failed to provide any scientific basis to validate the practice. Those who believe, however, claim that the divining rod is animated by the presence of an underground water or mineral source. But careful observation has shown that the agitation of the instrument is due to slight muscular movements of the person, which may be subconscious, but are certainly not "magical."

20 Diviners also feel that their talent to locate hidden objects is a special psychic gift. Scientists sympathetic to their cause say that diviners are actually responding to electromagnetic currents beneath the earth's surface which indicate the presence of minerals or water. Skeptics have a different explanation. They note that diviners usually work on land that they know well and are familiar with all the signs, nature's visual clues that suggest the presence of water in an area.

31. The author's attitude toward divining is best described as
   (A) informative
   (B) hostile
   (C) amused
   (D) positive
   (E) enthusiastic

32. According to the passage, divining may involve all of the following EXCEPT
   (A) magic
   (B) visual clues
   (C) a psychic gift
   (D) popular practice
   (E) electromagnetic currents

33. Which of the following best describes a diviner?
   (A) sinner
   (B) mystic
   (C) skeptic
   (D) scientist
   (E) explorer

34. The objective of the diviner is to
   (A) strike rocks
   (B) perform magic
   (C) pick up signals from water and minerals
   (D) discover underground water or minerals
   (E) find wood that has special location properties

35. It is most reasonable to infer from the passage that
   (A) divining is a religious practice
   (B) diviners are obsolete practitioners
   (C) wood has special locational properties
   (D) underground water sends electromagnetic signals
   (E) divining is somewhat successful since it continues to be used

GO ON TO THE NEXT PAGE.

On the 31st of August, 1846, I left Concord in Massachusetts for Bangor and the backwoods of Maine, by way of the railroad and steamboat. I was intending to accompany a relative of mine engaged in the lumber-trade in Bangor, as far as a dam on the west branch of the Penobscot, in which property he was interested. From this

Line 5　place, which is about one hundred miles by the river above Bangor, thirty miles from the Houlton military road, and five miles beyond the last log-hut, I proposed to make excursions to Mount Ktaadn, the second highest mountain in New England, about thirty miles distant, and to some of the lakes of the Penobscot, either alone or with such company as I might pick up there. It is unusual to find a camp so far in the woods at

10　that season, when lumbering operations have ceased. I was glad to avail myself of the circumstance of a gang of men being employed there at that time repairing the injuries caused by the great freshet in the spring. The mountain may be approached more easily and directly on horseback and on foot from the northeast side, by the Aroostook road, and the Wassataquoik River, but in that case you see much less of the wilderness, none

15　of the glorious river and lake scenery, and have no experience of the *batteau* and the boat man's life. I was fortunate also in the season of the year. In the summer myriads of black flies, mosquitoes, and midges make travelling in the woods almost impossible; but now their reign was nearly over.

36. Which of the following events mentioned in the passage occurred in the spring?

   (A) The author met his relative.
   (B) There were damaging floods.
   (C) The author travelled by train.
   (D) Insects interfered with travel.
   (E) Lumbering operations ceased.

37. In the context of the passage, you can tell that a "*batteau*" (line 15) is most likely

   (A) a boat
   (B) a road
   (C) a freshet
   (D) an insect
   (E) a wilderness

38. From the details, you can tell that the author is happy to be traveling in the fall because he

   (A) prefers to travel by himself
   (B) fears spending time with lumberjacks
   (C) wants to travel after the lumbering season
   (D) plans to avoid spending time with his relative
   (E) has chosen to travel when insects are scarce

39. How did the author feel when he encountered a group of men working in the woods?

   (A) quite angry
   (B) extremely excited
   (C) somewhat fearful
   (D) mildly interested
   (E) pleasantly surprised

40. The author's main purpose in writing this passage is most likely to

   (A) describe his travels
   (B) persuade readers to travel
   (C) criticize his relative's career choice
   (D) compare travel by railroad and steamboat
   (E) explain the dangers of lumbering operations

STOP
IF YOU FINISH BEFORE TIME IS CALLED,
YOU MAY CHECK YOUR WORK ON THIS SECTION ONLY.
DO NOT TURN TO ANY OTHER SECTION IN THE TEST.

SECTION 3
60 Questions

This section consists of two different types of questions: synonyms and analogies. There are directions and a sample question for each type.

Synonyms

Each of the following questions consists of one word followed by five words or phrases. You are to select the one word or phrase whose meaning is closest to the word in capital letters.

Sample Question:

> CHILLY:
>
> (A) lazy
> (B) nice
> (C) dry
> (D) cold
> (E) sunny
>
> Ⓐ Ⓑ Ⓒ ● Ⓔ

---

1. TRADITIONAL:
   (A) sensible
   (B) practical
   (C) erroneous
   (D) customary
   (E) concerning

2. EXPLORE:
   (A) hike
   (B) shuffle
   (C) search
   (D) furnish
   (E) conceal

3. DEBATE:
   (A) spar
   (B) elect
   (C) agree
   (D) reject
   (E) review

4. BOISTEROUS:
   (A) obvious
   (B) glorious
   (C) stupendous
   (D) contiguous
   (E) uproarious

5. SOLVE:
   (A) guess at
   (B) work out
   (C) shake off
   (D) concern for
   (E) speak about

6. TREMBLE:
   (A) fear
   (B) erase
   (C) shake
   (D) tumble
   (E) plaster

7. AUTHORITY:
   (A) coach
   (B) talent
   (C) expert
   (D) worker
   (E) relative

8. BOLSTER:
   (A) help
   (B) admit
   (C) succeed
   (D) organize
   (E) intervene

GO ON TO THE NEXT PAGE.

9. FLEDGLING:
   (A) ideal
   (B) newcomer
   (C) professional
   (D) opponent
   (E) mentor

10. OPULENT:
    (A) fervor
    (B) tender
    (C) callow
    (D) affluent
    (E) diminutive

11. ILLUMINATION:
    (A) sign
    (B) failing
    (C) miracle
    (D) lighting
    (E) sensation

12. FALLACY:
    (A) joke
    (B) religion
    (C) mistake
    (D) problem
    (E) accident

13. COMPREHENSIBLE:
    (A) understandable
    (B) confusing
    (C) different
    (D) removed
    (E) secured

14. SEVER:
    (A) cut off
    (B) turn out
    (C) put away
    (D) go forward
    (E) make difficult

15. SYNTHESIS:
    (A) position
    (B) doctrine
    (C) thesaurus
    (D) combination
    (E) malfeasance

16. PILOT:
    (A) steer
    (B) cruise
    (C) follow
    (D) conspire
    (E) terminate

17. BELLICOSE:
    (A) tedious
    (B) combative
    (C) uniformed
    (D) celebratory
    (E) international

18. PESTER:
    (A) trap
    (B) grip
    (C) ring
    (D) catch
    (E) bother

19. CLINCH:
    (A) clank
    (B) finish
    (C) secure
    (D) release
    (E) rewind

20. LISTLESSNESS:
    (A) neatness
    (B) deafness
    (C) loneliness
    (D) sluggishness
    (E) awkwardness

GO ON TO THE NEXT PAGE.

21. DEBILITATE:
    (A) split
    (B) annoy
    (C) pinch
    (D) weaken
    (E) measure

22. COMPASSION:
    (A) disgust
    (B) gratitude
    (C) silence
    (D) relief
    (E) pity

23. ADORN:
    (A) circulate
    (B) spill
    (C) decorate
    (D) tempt
    (E) embrace

24. TIRESOME:
    (A) irritating
    (B) gentle
    (C) small
    (D) active
    (E) huge

25. SUBTLE:
    (A) casual
    (B) obvious
    (C) subtitled
    (D) understated
    (E) anachronistic

26. PRESERVE:
    (A) abuse
    (B) watch
    (C) replace
    (D) exploit
    (E) maintain

27. RANK:
    (A) stripe
    (B) posture
    (C) element
    (D) standing
    (E) temperate

28. PETITE:
    (A) tall
    (B) tiny
    (C) crisp
    (D) simple
    (E) pleasant

29. IMPERTINENT:
    (A) aloof
    (B) gaudy
    (C) humble
    (D) shamefaced
    (E) presumptuous

30. VETTED:
    (A) blessed
    (B) soiled
    (C) clothed
    (D) examined
    (E) fabricated

GO ON TO THE NEXT PAGE.

Analogies

The following questions ask you to find relationships between words. For each question, select the answer choice that best completes the meaning of the sentence.

Sample Question:

> Kitten is to cat as
> (A) fawn is to colt
> (B) puppy is to dog
> (C) cow is to bull
> (D) wolf is to bear
> (E) hen is to rooster   Ⓐ   Ⓒ Ⓓ Ⓔ

Choice (B) is the best answer because a kitten is a young cat just as a puppy is a young dog. Of all the answer choices, (B) states a relationship that is most like the relationship between kitten and cat.

---

31. Acrid is to smell as

    (A) sour is to taste
    (B) robust is to touch
    (C) fuzzy is to hearing
    (D) elated is to emotion
    (E) cacophony is to sight

32. Dish is to platter as placemat is to

    (A) tray
    (B) sheet
    (C) towel
    (D) placard
    (E) tablecloth

33. Needle is to stitching as

    (A) scissors is to securing
    (B) bolt is to turning
    (C) piano is to singing
    (D) window is to seeing
    (E) brush is to painting

34. Flexibility is to agility as sleuth is to

    (A) sloth
    (B) sculptor
    (C) gymnast
    (D) embezzler
    (E) investigator

35. Rind is to grapefruit as

    (A) husk is to corn
    (B) box is to flour
    (C) fuzz is to peach
    (D) pit is to cherry
    (E) pork is to sausage

36. Shelve is to forward as

    (A) rush is to hurry
    (B) store is to retreat
    (C) hold is to advance
    (D) delay is to contain
    (E) movement is to progress

37. Fleece is to llama as

    (A) fur is to coat
    (B) wool is to rug
    (C) feathers is to hat
    (D) coop is to pigeon
    (E) down is to duckling

38. Illness is to epidemic as

    (A) horse is to herd
    (B) window is to view
    (C) wave is to tsunami
    (D) darkness is to night
    (E) poverty is to bankruptcy

GO ON TO THE NEXT PAGE.

39. Apology is to acknowledgment as
    (A) admittance is to lie
    (B) avoidance is to blame
    (C) confession is to teacher
    (D) excuse is to justification
    (E) scheme is to presumption

40. Adversary is to enmity as underdog is to
    (A) folly
    (B) sympathy
    (C) hospitality
    (D) gratefulness
    (E) connectivity

41. Haunting is to nightmare as throbbing is to
    (A) poetry
    (B) thriller
    (C) runner
    (D) massage
    (E) headache

42. Telescope is to astronomer as stethoscope is to
    (A) chemist
    (B) patient
    (C) biologist
    (D) physician
    (E) mechanic

43. Gasoline is to engines as
    (A) light is to mirrors
    (B) steam is to turbines
    (C) water is to fountains
    (D) electricity is to wires
    (E) smoke is to chimneys

44. Tempest is to storm as
    (A) hurricane is to hail
    (B) tsunami is to ocean
    (C) conflagration is to fire
    (D) lightning is to thunder
    (E) whirlpool is to maelstrom

45. Preface is to speech as
    (A) label is to file
    (B) door is to garage
    (C) address is to letter
    (D) issue is to magazine
    (E) homepage is to website

46. Principle is to philosopher as
    (A) creation is to job
    (B) idea is to student
    (C) fantasy is to movie
    (D) topic is to paragraph
    (E) presumption is to detective

47. Resistant is to obstinate as
    (A) tome is to book
    (B) eager is to easy
    (C) thrilled is to glad
    (D) fertile is to ingenious
    (E) aggressive is to animal

48. Helium is to nitrogen as
    (A) marble is to rock
    (B) methane is to gas
    (C) steam is to vapor
    (D) smoke is to fumes
    (E) hydrogen is to oxygen

49. Button is to collar as
    (A) lock is to key
    (B) cuff is to coat
    (C) link is to chain
    (D) clasp is to purse
    (E) sash is to uniform

50. Hurricane is to squall as
    (A) puff is to gust
    (B) claw is to talon
    (C) clap is to clatter
    (D) funnel is to cloud
    (E) torrent is to drizzle

GO ON TO THE NEXT PAGE.

51. Tree is to forest as
    - (A) ship is to fleet
    - (B) turn is to road
    - (C) gap is to canyon
    - (D) circus is to clown
    - (E) herd is to elephant

52. Mischief is to kindness as disobedience is to
    - (A) elegant
    - (B) conflict
    - (C) flattering
    - (D) conformity
    - (E) suppression

53. Ask is to order as
    - (A) advise is to hint
    - (B) dark is to black
    - (C) nonsense is to babble
    - (D) appeal is to command
    - (E) request is to propose

54. Discern is to perceive as
    - (A) hear is to testify
    - (B) judge is to justify
    - (C) see is to witness
    - (D) digress is to trespass
    - (E) ascertain is to determine

55. Unpleasant is to detestable as
    - (A) kindly is to gentle
    - (B) nervous is to anxious
    - (C) thin is to emaciated
    - (D) adequate is to average
    - (E) probable is to possible

56. Trademark is to brand as
    - (A) sale is to store
    - (B) register is to vote
    - (C) certificate is to gift
    - (D) repair is to damage
    - (E) copyright is to book

57. Sufficient is to plentiful as
    - (A) inactive is to idle
    - (B) peculiar is to odd
    - (C) adequate is to lavish
    - (D) elaborate is to fancy
    - (E) seldom is to occasional

58. Smile is to laugh as
    - (A) wink is to nod
    - (B) frown is to cry
    - (C) scream is to whisper
    - (D) blink is to smirk
    - (E) giggle is to yawn

59. Reproduce is to experiment as
    - (A) cast is to sculpture
    - (B) design is to garment
    - (C) fabricate is to product
    - (D) assemble is to machine
    - (E) reconstruct is to building

60. Fuzzy is to thinking as
    - (A) foggy is to river
    - (B) downy is to goose
    - (C) hazy is to memory
    - (D) damp is to basement
    - (E) trim is to appearance

STOP
**IF YOU FINISH BEFORE TIME IS CALLED,
YOU MAY CHECK YOUR WORK ON THIS SECTION ONLY.
DO NOT TURN TO ANY OTHER SECTION IN THE TEST.**

SECTION 4
25 Questions

Following each problem in this section, there are five suggested answers. Work each problem in your head or in the blank space provided at the right of the page. Then look at the five suggested answers and decide which one is best.

<u>Note:</u> Figures that accompany problems in this section are drawn as accurately as possible EXCEPT when it is stated in a specific problem that its figure is not drawn to scale.

Sample Problem:

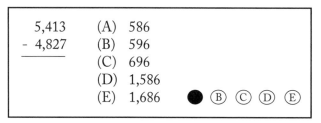

```
  5,413    (A)  586
- 4,827    (B)  596
_____    (C)  696
           (D)  1,586
           (E)  1,686    ● Ⓑ Ⓒ Ⓓ Ⓔ
```

---

1. When 6,508 is divided by 201, the result is closest to which of the following?

   (A) 20
   (B) 25
   (C) 30
   (D) 40
   (E) 50

USE THIS SPACE FOR FIGURING.

---

2. If $16 \times S = 16$, then $16 + S =$

   (A) 0
   (B) $\frac{1}{16}$
   (C) 1
   (D) 16
   (E) 17

---

3. $100 - 19\frac{2}{3} =$

   (A) $80\frac{1}{3}$
   (B) $80\frac{2}{3}$
   (C) $80\frac{5}{6}$
   (D) $81\frac{1}{3}$
   (E) $81\frac{5}{6}$

GO ON TO THE NEXT PAGE.

USE THIS SPACE FOR FIGURING.

4. Six equal pieces are cut from a piece of lumber 88 inches long. How long is the leftover piece?

   (A) 2"
   (B) 4"
   (C) 8"
   (D) 14"
   (E) 38"

5. 0.075 × 20.00 =

   (A) 0.015
   (B) 0.15
   (C) 1.5
   (D) 15
   (E) 150

6. Calculate $2x - y^2$ when $x = 5$ and $y = 3$.

   (A) 1
   (B) 4
   (C) 0
   (D) 6
   (E) 15

7. $3\frac{2}{3} + 4\frac{1}{3} + 3\frac{2}{3} =$

   (A) 11.33
   (B) 11.67
   (C) 12.06
   (D) 12.33
   (E) 12.67

8. There are 20 boys and 30 girls in a class. Two-thirds of the girls are wearing blue shirts. Seventy-five percent of the boys are wearing green shirts. How many more students are wearing blue shirts?

   (A) 5
   (B) 10
   (C) 15
   (D) 20
   (E) 35

GO ON TO THE NEXT PAGE.

127

USE THIS SPACE FOR FIGURING.

9. Evaluate: $(-18) + (-12) + 44$

(A) -74
(B) -14
(C) 14
(D) 44
(E) 74

10. 44 is 8 percent of

(A) 88
(B) 220
(C) 330
(D) 440
(E) 550

11. The perimeter of an octagon is 20 units. If the length of each side of the figure is increased by 2 units, what is the perimeter of the new figure?

(A) 22
(B) 28
(C) 30
(D) 36
(E) 40

12. Ms. Walinsky paid $1,800 for a rectangular field 200 feet wide and 300 feet long. What was her cost per square foot?

(A) $3.00
(B) $0.30
(C) $1.70
(D) $0.03
(E) $60.00

GO ON TO THE NEXT PAGE.

USE THIS SPACE FOR FIGURING.

13. Choose the inequality represented by the statement: "The sum of three times a number and four times another number is greater than or equal to twenty-seven."

    (A) $3a \times 4b \geq 27$

    (B) $3a \times 4b \leq 27$

    (C) $3a + 4a \geq 27$

    (D) $3a + 4b \leq 27$

    (E) $3a + 4b \geq 27$

14. A taxi driver took between $1\frac{1}{2}$ and 2 hours to make a 60-mile trip. The average speed, in miles per hour, must have been between

    (A) 10 and 20

    (B) 20 and 25

    (C) 25 and 30

    (D) 30 and 40

    (E) 40 and 50

15. The average time for each leg of a three-leg bus journey took Tom four hours and four minutes. How long did it take Tom to complete the journey?

    (A) 10 hours and 24 minutes

    (B) 11 hours and 36 minutes

    (C) 12 hours

    (D) 12 hours and 12 minutes

    (E) 13 hours

16. What percentage of the figure shown is shaded?

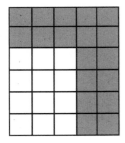

    (A) 12%

    (B) 18%

    (C) 40%

    (D) 55%

    (E) 60%

GO ON TO THE NEXT PAGE.

USE THIS SPACE FOR FIGURING.

17. $3 \overline{)723}$ =

(A) $\frac{700}{3} \times \frac{20}{3} \times \frac{3}{3}$

(B) $\frac{700}{3} + \frac{20}{3} + \frac{3}{3}$

(C) $\frac{70}{3} + \frac{23}{3}$

(D) $\frac{700}{3} + 23$

(E) $\frac{7}{3} + \frac{2}{3} + \frac{3}{3}$

18. What is the value of the underlined digit? 927.$\underline{6}$4

(A) 6 hundredths

(B) 6 tenths

(C) 6 ones

(D) 6 tens

(E) 6 oneths

19. Which of the following gives the number of cents in
x nickels, y quarters, and 4 pennies?

(A) $\frac{x}{5} + \frac{y}{25} + 4$

(B) $\frac{5}{x} + \frac{25}{y} + 4$

(C) $5x + 5y + 1$

(D) $5x + 25y + 4$

(E) $5x + y + 100$

20. How many yards of fencing are needed to enclose a
14-yard-long by 8-yard-wide garden?

(A) 22 yards

(B) 42 yards

(C) 44 yards

(D) 152 yards

(E) 252 yards

GO ON TO THE NEXT PAGE.

USE THIS SPACE FOR FIGURING.

21. Let h represent the height of a rectangle. Which expression would represent the perimeter of this rectangle if the base is 7 less than the height?

    (A) $h^2 + 7h$

    (B) $4h - 14$

    (C) $2h - 7$

    (D) $h^2 + 7$

    (E) $4h + 14$

22. If $a + b$ is divisible by 11, which of the following is also divisible by 11?

    (A) $(a \times b) + 11$

    (B) $a + (11 \times b)$

    (C) $(11 \times a) + b$

    (D) $(2 \times a) + (2 \times b)$

    (E) $\dfrac{a - b}{11}$

23. In a survey, each of 300 students was found to own a car, a bike, or both. If 200 of these students own cars and 200 own bikes, how many students own both a car and a bike?

    (A) 75

    (B) 100

    (C) 150

    (D) 200

    (E) 300

GO ON TO THE NEXT PAGE.

USE THIS SPACE FOR FIGURING.

24. Three roommates each contribute $4 per week to a savings fund for a TV for their apartment. How much would each person pay per week if a fourth roommate also contributed?

    (A) $1
    (B) $2
    (C) $3
    (D) $4
    (E) $12

---

25. If x is a whole number greater than 1, which of the following is least?

    (A) $\dfrac{x}{(x+1)}$

    (B) $x + 1$

    (C) $x - 1$

    (D) $2x + 1$

    (E) $x + \dfrac{1}{x}$

STOP

**IF YOU FINISH BEFORE TIME IS CALLED,
YOU MAY CHECK YOUR WORK ON THIS SECTION ONLY.
DO NOT TURN TO ANY OTHER SECTION IN THE TEST.**

Evaluating Your Upper Level SSAT

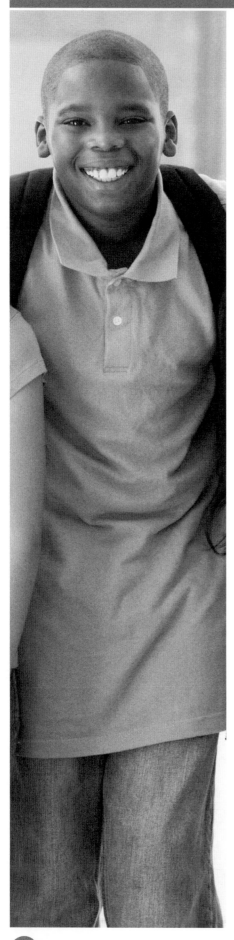

How Did You Do?

When you have completed the practice tests, give yourself a pat on the back, and then take a few moments to think about your performance.

- Did you leave many questions unanswered?
- Did you run out of time?
- Did you read the directions carefully?

Based on your understanding of how well you performed, review the particular test sections that gave you difficulty. Remember, the practice tests are only used for *practice*.

Scoring the Practice Tests

In order to calculate your "raw score" (right, wrong, and omitted answers) for each test section, use the answer keys on pages 136-141. The *Official Guide to the Upper Level SSAT* contains practice tests, not "retired" forms of the test. These tests are intended to familiarize you with the format, content, and timing of the actual test. These tests do not provide you with a score as if you were taking the actual SSAT.

Computing Your Raw Score

1. Using the Practice Test Answer Keys found on pages 136-141, check your answer sheet against the list of correct answers.

2. Mark your answer for each test question in the "Your Answer" column. Next, give yourself a ✓ in the "C" column for each correct answer, a **0** for each wrong answer in the "W" column, and a — for each question omitted in the "O" column.

Correct Answer	Your Answer	C ✓	W 0	O —
1. A	A	✓		
2. B	C		0	
3. C				–
4. C	C	✓		
5. D	D	✓		

3. Add the total number of correct answers and enter the number in the "Total # Correct" box; add the number of **0**s and enter in the "Total # Wrong" box. (It is not necessary to add the number of omits. You can use that information to go back and review those questions and to make sure that you understand all answers.)

4. Raw scores are calculated by using the following system:

• One point is given for each correct answer.

• No points are added or subtracted for questions omitted.

• One-fourth of a point is subtracted from the number of correct answers for each incorrect answer.

5. Divide the number of wrong answers in the "Total # Wrong" box by 4 and enter the number in the "# Wrong ÷ 4" box. For example, if you had 32 right and 19 wrong, then your raw score is 32 minus one fourth of 19, which equals $27\frac{1}{4}$ ($32 - 4\frac{3}{4} = 27\frac{1}{4}$).

Total # Correct:	1
Total # Wrong:	
# Wrong ÷ 4:	2
Box 1 - Box 2	3
Round Box 3 to nearest whole integer:	4
Raw Score:	

6. Round the result in box 3 to the nearest whole integer. Put the integer in Box 4. For example, round $27\frac{1}{4}$ to 27.

7. The integer in Box 4 is the raw score on the section.

8. Repeat this procedure for each simulated test section that you have taken.

Answer Key

Upper Level Practice Test I : QUANTITATIVE (Sections 1 and 4)

For each question, mark ✓ if correct (C), **0** if wrong (W), or – if omitted (O).

Correct Answer	Your Answer	C ✓	W 0	O –
Section 1				
1. C	C	✓		
2. E	E	✓		
3. C	C	✓		
4. B	B	✓		
5. B	B	✓		
6. D	A			O
7. E	E	✓		
8. B				–
9. A				–
10. D				–
11. E	B		O	
12. D	C		O	
13. A	B		O	
14. B	B	✓		
15. E	C		O	
16. D	D	✓		
17. C	C	✓		
18. B	B	✓		
19. E				–
20. D	C		O	
21. D	D	✓		
22. C				–
23. B	C		O	
24. C				–
25. B				–
Subtotal		11	7	7

Correct Answer	Your Answer	C ✓	W 0	O –
Section 4				
1. A	A	✓		
2. E	E	✓		
3. A	A	✓		
4. E	E	✓		
5. C	C	✓		
6. E				–
7. D	C		O	
8. D				–
9. E	E	✓		
10. B				–
11. B	B	✓		
12. E	E	✓		
13. A				–
14. B				–
15. D				–
16. D	E		O	
17. B	B	✓		
18. E				–
19. D				–
20. B				–
21. D	D	✓		
22. C	D		O	
23. B	B	✓		
24. D	C		O	
25. A	A	✓		
Subtotal		12	4	9

Total # Correct:	22
Total # Wrong:	11
# Wrong ÷ 4:	3
Box 1 - Box 2:	19
Round Box 3 to nearest whole integer:	19

Quantitative Raw Score: 19
Box 4

Quantitative Estimated Scaled Score:
See Table on page 142

Answer Key

Upper Level Practice Test 1 : READING (Section 2)

For each question, mark ✓ if correct (C), **0** if wrong (W), or − if omitted (O).

Correct Answer	Your Answer	C ✓	W 0	O −
1. E	E	✓		
2. E	E	✓		
3. B	A		✓	
4. C	C	✓		
5. D	D	✓		
6. B	A		✓	
7. E	E	✓		
8. C	C	✓		
9. B	−			✓
10. D	D	✓		
11. A	A	✓		
12. D	A		✓	
13. D	A		✓	
14. E	E	✓		
15. B	B	✓		
16. A	C		✓	
17. D	E		✓	
18. A	A	✓		
19. E	−			✓
20. C	C	✓		

Correct Answer	Your Answer	C ✓	W 0	O −
21. C	E		✓	
22. D	D	✓		
23. E	A		✓	
24. C	A		✓	
25. B	−			✓
26. B	A		✓	
27. A	E		✓	
28. A	C		✓	
29. B	E		✓	
30. D	D	✓		
31. B	B	✓		
32. C	C	✓		
33. A	A	✓		
34. D	−			✓
35. C	E		✓	
36. A	A		✓	
37. D	−			✓
38. A	−			✓
39. C	C	✓		
40. E	E	✓		

Total # Correct:	¹ 19
Total # Wrong:	14
# Wrong ÷ 4:	² 3.5
Box 1 - Box 2	³ 15.5
Round Box 3 to nearest whole integer:	⁴ 16

Reading Raw Score: 16

Box 4

Reading Estimated Scaled Score:

See Table on page 142

Answer Key

Upper Level Practice Test I : VERBAL (Section 3)

For each question, mark ✓ if correct (C), **0** if wrong (W), or – if omitted (O).

Correct Answer	Your Answer	C ✓	W 0	O –
1. E				
2. A				
3. C				
4. C				
5. D				
6. B				
7. A				
8. E				
9. C				
10. B				
11. D				
12. A				
13. C				
14. D				
15. E				
16. B				
17. D				
18. E				
19. E				
20. D				
21. B				
22. D				
23. C				
24. D				
25. C				
26. C				
27. D				
28. E				
29. D				
30. C				
Subtotal				

Correct Answer	Your Answer	C ✓	W 0	O –
31. D				
32. C				
33. B				
34. C				
35. E				
36. E				
37. B				
38. B				
39. E				
40. A				
41. D				
42. D				
43. A				
44. C				
45. C				
46. A				
47. C				
48. B				
49. C				
50. C				
51. A				
52. A				
53. E				
54. E				
55. A				
56. C				
57. D				
58. D				
59. E				
60. D				
Subtotal				

Total # Correct:	1
Total # Wrong:	
# Wrong ÷ 4:	2
Box 1 - Box 2	3
Round Box 3 to nearest whole integer:	4

Verbal Raw Score:

Box 4

Verbal Estimated Scaled Score:

See Table on page 142

Answer Key

Upper Level Practice Test II : QUANTITATIVE (Sections 1 and 4)

For each question, mark ✓ if correct (C), **0** if wrong (W), or – if omitted (O).

Correct Answer	Your Answer	C ✓	W 0	O –
Section 1				
1. C	C	✓		
2. B	B	✓		
3. E	E	✓		
4. C	D			O
5. A	A	✓		
6. D	D	✓		
7. E	E	✓		
8. D	D	✓		
9. E	E	✓		
10. C	C	✓		
11. E	E	✓		
12. B	B	✓		
13. A	A	✓		
14. C	A			O
15. E	E	✓		
16. E	E	✓		
17. A	C			O
18. C	A			O
19. B	D			O
20. A				–
21. E	C			O
22. B	B	✓		
23. B	A			O
24. C				–
25. B				–
Subtotal		15	7	3

Correct Answer	Your Answer	C ✓	W 0	O –
Section 4				
1. C	C	✓		
2. E	E	✓		
3. A	A	✓		
4. B	B	✓		
5. C	C	✓		
6. A	A	✓		
7. B	B	✓		
8. A	A	✓		
9. C	C	✓		
10. E	E	✓		
11. D	D	✓		
12. D	B			O
13. E	E	✓		
14. D	D	✓		
15. D	D	✓		
16. E	E	✓		
17. B	B	✓		
18. B	B	✓		
19. D	D	✓		
20. C	C	✓		
21. B	B	✓		
22. D	D	✓		
23. B	B	✓		
24. C	C	✓		
25. A	A	✓		
Subtotal		24	1	0

Total # Correct:	[1] 39
Total # Wrong:	8
# Wrong ÷ 4:	[2] 2
Box 1 - Box 2	[3] 37
Round Box 3 to nearest whole integer:	[4] 37

Quantitative Raw Score: 37
Box 4

Quantitative Estimated Scaled Score:
See Table on page 142

Answer Key

Upper Level Practice Test II : READING (Section 2)

For each question, mark ✓ if correct (C), **0** if wrong (W), or − if omitted (O).

Correct Answer	Your Answer	C ✓	W 0	O −
1. E	E	✓		
2. D	D	✓		
3. B	D		0	
4. A	C		0	
5. E	A		0	
6. E	E	✓		
7. B	B	✓		
8. A	A	✓		
9. D	D	✓		
10. D	E		0	
11. E	A		0	
12. C	E		0	
13. B	B	✓		
14. D	A		0	
15. B	B	✓		
16. B				−
17. A	A	✓		
18. A	A	✓		
19. E	E	✓		
20. D	E		0	

Correct Answer	Your Answer	C ✓	W 0	O −
21. A	A	✓		
22. A	D		0	
23. C	B		0	
24. D				−
25. B	B	✓		
26. B	B	✓		
27. D	C		0	
28. C	C	✓		
29. B	B	✓		
30. B	A		0	
31. A		✓		−
32. A	A	✓		
33. B	E		0	
34. D	D		0	
35. E	E	✓		
36. B	E		0	
37. A	A	✓		
38. E	E	✓		
39. E	C		0	
40. A	C		0	

Total # Correct:	¹ 20
Total # Wrong:	17
# Wrong ÷ 4:	² 4.25
Box 1 - Box 2	³ 15.75
Round Box 3 to nearest whole integer:	⁴ 16

Reading Raw Score: 16

Box 4

Reading Estimated Scaled Score:

See Table on page 142

Answer Key

Upper Level Practice Test II : VERBAL (Section 3)

For each question, mark ✓ if correct (C), **0** if wrong (W), or – if omitted (O).

Correct Answer	Your Answer	C ✓	W 0	O –
1. D	D	✓		
2. C	C	✓		
3. A	D		0	
4. E	E	✓		
5. B	B	✓		
6. C	C	✓		
7. C	A		0	
8. A				–
9. B				–
10. D				–
11. D	D	✓		
12. C	C	✓		
13. A	A	✓		
14. A	A	✓		
15. D	D	✓		
16. A	A	✓		
17. B	B	✓		
18. E	E	✓		
19. C	B		0	
20. D	C		0	
21. D	D	✓		
22. E	B		0	
23. C	C	✓		
24. A	A	✓		
25. D	A		0	
26. E	E	✓		
27. D	D	✓		
28. B	B		0	
29. E				–
30. D	D	✓		
Subtotal		19	7	4

Correct Answer	Your Answer	C ✓	W 0	O –
31. A	E		0	
32. E	E	✓		
33. E	E	✓		
34. E	D		0	
35. A	A	✓		
36. C	E		0	
37. E	E	✓		
38. C	C	✓		
39. D	D	✓		
40. B				–
41. E	E	✓		
42. D	D	✓		
43. B	D		0	
44. C	C	✓		
45. E				–
46. E	A		0	
47. C	C	✓		
48. E	E	✓		
49. D	D	✓		
50. E				–
51. A	D		0	
52. D	A		0	
53. D				–
54. E				–
55. C	B		0	
56. E	E	✓		
57. C	B		0	
58. B	B	✓		
59. E	E	✓		
60. C	C	✓		
Subtotal		16	9	5

Total # Correct:	1. 34
Total # Wrong:	17
# Wrong ÷ 4:	2. 4.25
Box 1 - Box 2:	3. 29.75
Round Box 3 to nearest whole integer:	4. 30

Verbal Raw Score: 30

Box 4

Verbal Estimated Scaled Score:

See Table on page 142

Equating Raw Scores to Scaled Scores

Scores are first calculated by awarding one point for each correct answer and subtracting one-quarter of one point for each incorrect answer. These scores are called raw scores. Raw scores can vary from one edition of the test to another due to differences in difficulty among editions. A statistical procedure called "equating" is used to adjust for these differences. Even after these adjustments, no single test score provides a perfectly accurate estimate of your proficiency.

Because the *Official Guide to the Upper Level SSAT* guide contains practice tests and not "retired" forms of the test, there are no norms associated with these forms, and calculations of exact scaled scores or specific percentile rankings are not possible. But the following chart will give you a good estimate of where your scaled scores might fall within each of the three scored sections: Verbal, Quantitative/Math, and Reading. These tests are intended to familiarize you with the format, content, and timing of the test and to approximate a potential scaled score.

Table: Upper Level Estimated SSAT Scaled Scores			
Raw Score	**Estimated Verbal Scaled Score**	**Estimated Quantitative Scaled Score**	**Estimated Reading Scaled Score**
60	800		
55	800		
50	791	800	
45	767	790	
40	741	764	800
35	717	740	745
30	692	716	711
25	667	692	681
20	641	667	651
15	615	640	619
10	586	610	586
5	556	578	553
0	525	544	522
-5	501	512	503

These are estimated scaled scores based on the raw-to-scaled conversion of many forms, and a student's score can vary when taking the test.

Notes

Notes